Contents

Foreword

An amazing fundraiser, motivator, brand builder, networker, dinner guest, TV star, companion, a wether from the back of Bendigo, a sheep called Shrek.

Little did we realise the impact Shrek would have on Cure Kids. We had no idea how the Shrek opportunity was going to evolve. How could anyone? There had never been anything like it in New Zealand. A long-lost sheep as a brand builder — preposterous!

Yet when John and Heather offered to make Cure Kids Shrek's charity of choice we were honoured to have been chosen. It was an easy decision to say yes.

As the public face of the Child Health Research Foundation, the Cure Kids brand was only four years old when Shrek arrived. While we were well recognised in the corporate world our public awareness was limited. Shrek, as our first four-legged celebrity ambassador, quickly changed that. John and Heather never hesitated to fly or drive Shrek anywhere in New Zealand to personally represent Cure Kids at a local fundraiser. They were a formidable combo.

Shrek, ranked as one of the top news stories on CNN and BBC, generated publicity that money simply could not buy. Our ambassador raised significant funds for the Cure Kids capital campaign to fund the Cure Kids Chair of Child Health Research at the University of Otago in Dunedin.

Shrek has had his share of critics but for every one of those there have been thousands who have embraced the Shrek journey for what it is — an incredible opportunity to be part of something that has no commercial gain, no hidden message. Quite simply, it's a feel-good story about a woolly wether with an inspirational owner whose journey captivated the attention of the world.

The Shrek journey is far from over and who knows what John's next adventure will be. Sadly Heather won't be there to share this and relive the exaggerated Shrek stories. But we know John still feels Heather with him on this journey and her spirit is very much alive in our hearts. John, your and Heather's generosity, leadership, vision and self-belief has been a treasured gift. A gift that will forever be remembered.

Roy Austin
Chairman

Introduction

As the Air New Zealand jet throttled back over the top of the Lindis Pass and started the long glide south into Queenstown, I looked out the window at the mountains and vast basin of the Upper Clutha. From 30,000 feet the land looked dry and barren, contrasting with the blue of Lake Wanaka and Lake Hawea feeding the mighty Clutha River, weaving like a snake down into Lake Dunstan at Cromwell.

Then, over the intercom, came the familiar message: 'Please fasten your seatbelts, put your seats in the upright position and put your tray tables away.' I knew that in a few more minutes I would step off the plane, along with tourists from all around the world. There, smack right in front of us, would be the spectacle of the Remarkable mountains, offering an emotional welcome to the grandeur of New Zealand's high country.

New Zealand is a very small country, but the contrasts and beauty of our South Pacific paradise never cease to amaze me. Our flight had left the Super City, Auckland, near the top of the North Island, a little over an hour before. As we'd headed south, the green hills, dense bush country and volcanoes of the North Island had given way to the rugged mountain ranges that form the backbone of the South Island.

As we started the approach to Queenstown I could see, far out on the left side of the plane, Castle Rock standing majestically on the top of Bendigo Station, home for me and also a celebrity hermit merino sheep called Shrek.

In 2004, Shrek had become an overnight phenomenon when he was discovered and captured after evading musterers for six years by hiding high up in the Central Otago mountains. For weeks the world's media had gone crazy over the giant woolly, and in the years that followed Shrek became a New Zealand icon as he travelled the country raising funds for charity.

Home is about an hour-long drive from Queenstown airport, through the

10 Shrek: The story of a Kiwi icon   **Above**: The kids at Paihia thought Shrek was 'pretty cool, eh'.

winding Kawarau Gorge to Cromwell, and then another 10 minutes north up the highway to Bendigo. As soon as I pull in the gate my usual routine is to let the dogs off and then visit his highness. As I walk up the steps to Shrek's house and push open the heavy sliding door to make an appearance, I know I'll get the Mexican stand-off silent treatment. The length of the wait will depend on how long I have been away from Bendigo. Eventually he will stamp his foot and his body language says it all: 'Where the bloody hell have you been without me?'

New Zealand is an animal-loving nation and it is no surprise that the kiwi is our national icon. This little brown flightless bird is extremely rare and unique. But ask any tourist or Aussie which animal they associate with New Zealand and they'll probably say the sheep. Not too many years ago, 60 million grazed our small island nation. This meant the sheep outnumbered every man, woman and child 20 times over.

The sheep population in New Zealand has shrunk by nearly half as we have diversified our land use and substantially increased the amount of land reserved for conservation. Today there are only about 30-odd million sheep left in New Zealand and, of them, Shrek, the famous woolly wether from Bendigo, has become an icon to a nation proud of our animal heritage. He also optimises our national love of pets, which sees most New Zealand homes include at least one animal as part of the family.

Our kiwi is defenceless to the predators introduced centuries ago, such as rats and stoats, and it is at

Above: Omarama schoolchildren pose with Shrek in front of a limestone merino statue.

great cost to our nation that the remaining birds are managed and protected in every way possible. Their future rests solely with New Zealand's Department of Conservation. Sheep, on the other hand, were introduced and have been managed as an economic resource from the time Europeans first started settling in New Zealand.

For many decades, Shrek's ancestors have provided meat and wool that have sustained a culture and lifestyle for New Zealanders over generations.

Sheep are managed with an extensive network of fencing throughout New Zealand and are moved between what we call paddocks or blocks by well-trained dogs, motorbikes and, more recently, helicopters. It seems they are always being chased or rounded up and they have subsequently developed an instinct to move away from what they see as danger, such as a dog. They also seek refuge and safety by staying together as a mob.

But Shrek has a very different approach to life. I have taken Shrek to many strange places in many strange ways and people continue to marvel at his assertiveness, confidence and lack of fear. He has no

Shrek has a very different approach to life. People continue to marvel at his assertiveness, confidence and lack of fear.

hesitation in travelling with me, be it in a stretch limo, helicopter or private jet, and this fascinates people of all ages, especially children. I have become known as the father of Shrek, and — as children often do — he has inherited my tendency to assert confidence in every situation.

A Japanese film crew was recently sent over to New Zealand to make a follow-up documentary about Shrek. They were absolutely amazed when Shrek walked through a mob of 1000 sheep in a very large paddock and showed no interest in joining his cousins. In fact, when a dog was introduced to hold the mob, he would run to me and stay very close. Shrek's nature and the trust he invests in humans is certainly unique and allows us to step outside the realms of normality and the stereotype of an everyday sheep.

This four-legged high country rebel, who seemed to think he was human and revelled in attention, captured the heart of the nation. As befits a celebrity, once captured, Shrek was moved into the luxurious Bendigo ram shed, which soon became known as the House of Shrek. He has never wanted for anything and has always demanded to be treated with the utmost respect. With the help of his human friends, he has enjoyed a hugely successful five-year career as a fundraiser, making frequent guest appearances to raise money for charity. Children's books have been written about him, he has met the prime minister, flown to an iceberg, and made an appearance in almost every corner of New Zealand. He has more frequent-flyer points than most New Zealanders. There was even a debate held: Is Shrek the real New Zealand idol? The answer was 'yes' although the opposition said he was only a 'nutless, gutless wether'!

At 14, Shrek is almost certainly the oldest sheep in New Zealand. Although officially retired now, by arrangement Shrek still welcomes all visitors except dogs. Corporate New Zealand is ready to oblige should he need a private jet or helicopter to travel somewhere to make an appearance.

Shrek's story is so unusual that people from all over

Above: The Ahuriri Valley and the road to Birchwood Station, the domain of Shrek's ancestors for over 100 years. Birchwood is now a conservation park and is still New Zealand at its very best.

New Zealand and (particularly) Australia are still having trouble getting their minds around the fact that it wasn't one of New Zealand's biggest jack-ups. They seem to believe he was a well-trained pet lamb that was planted in the hills for five years as a massive publicity stunt. Such is the power of envy. They even think he has been replaced by another younger version. There are only two of us in the world that know for sure. One is Shrek, who doesn't say a lot, and the other is me, the Father of Shrek. But his aloofness and old rock star arrogant manner is a total giveaway. There could never be two Shreks!

As the father of Shrek, I have been there for virtually every public appearance he has ever made. From the day he was found on the top of Bendigo, we have developed a special relationship. He doesn't need to say anything — I just know what he's thinking. The way he moves, listens and acknowledges people around him radiates his feelings towards them. Really, it's not a lot different from when I used to come home late from the pub. My late wife Heather didn't need to use words to get her point across. She didn't say anything — sometimes for a couple of days — but she sure got her point across!

The story of Shrek very much mirrors the story of New Zealand, the new-world country in which we live and of which we are so proud. My own ancestors sailed across the world from Scotland in pursuit of gold and a new life only 150 years ago. The hardships they, and their contemporaries, faced in an exciting but sometimes inhospitable and extreme climate in Central Otago cost the lives of many.

Big mountains and rivers with deep gorges had to be climbed and crossed in those early days to reach some of the world's richest gold deposits. Firstly, the gold seekers found alluvial gold at Gabriels Gully at Lawrence, not too far from Dunedin. Then on to Central Otago and Bendigo, which was the richest quartz reef strike in New Zealand.

Digging down to 150 metres through solid rock with not much more than their bare hands bred a hardy bunch of pioneers. They were lured from the old world of England and Scotland by the promise of prosperity. Few were to realise their dream and even fewer were able to sustain their wealth. One of New Zealand's wealthiest families, the Todd family, is one of the few success stories originating out of the goldfields at Bendigo, where they were mine managers.

Shrek's ancestors, on the other hand, migrated from North Africa many thousands of years ago into Central Europe with the Berber tribes. There they became the foundation of the world's textile industry and were so prized over centuries by kings and queens, it was an offence punishable by death to be caught exporting sheep to another country.

Eventually, Shrek's ancestors arrived in the country. Today, merino sheep can be found dotted all over the high country in the South Island and they still produce some of the world's whitest and softest wool, adopted by recognised brands such as Icebreaker, Untouched World and many more designer clothing labels, such as my daughter Christina's.

The day that Shrek was found on the top of Bendigo was the beginning of an incredible journey that has become part of New Zealand's story. That story you now hold in your hands.

John Perriam
Father of Shrek

Shrek, the Famous Sheep

Joy Cowley is one of New Zealand's most loved and respected writers. She started writing in the late 1960s to help one of her sons who had difficulty learning to read. In 1992 she was awarded an OBE for her services to children's literature. Quite unexpectedly, she penned this wonderful poem about Shrek. It has never before been published and takes poetic licence in places but is a gem just the same.

Shrek, the Famous Sheep

Joy Cowley

I'll tell you a story before you sleep,
About a famous merino sheep.
A sheep who was noble,
A sheep who was brave,
A sheep who lived in a mountain cave.
Now there's a medal around his neck
And on that medal is written SHREK.
The story begins several years ago,
With a little lamb that was born in snow.
He drank warm milk
From his mother ewe
And all that spring, he grew and grew.
He didn't know he was bound for fame
Or that he would get a much-loved name.
That summer the young sheep played together
And Shrek became a handsome wether.

Days were happy,
And nights were calm —
Until the wild dogs came to the farm.
They came in the dark without a sound,
Wild dogs creeping close to the ground.
The men in the farmhouse were fast asleep
When the dogs attacked the helpless sheep.
Shrek's heart beat fast,
He shook with fear,
A prowling, growling dog was near.
Shrek could smell the blood on its breath
And he knew he was facing certain death.
This was no time to freeze with fright,
Shrek turned and ran with all his might.
There was no escape,
The dog gave chase,
And they ran through the dark at a frantic pace.
Shrek was tired. His muscles were tense.
In front was the wire of the boundary fence.
When the big dog saw the wether pause,
It leapt with snarling, snapping jaws.
Shrek was stuck.
What could he do?
He jumped at the fence and went right through.
The dog couldn't follow, although it tried,
And Shrek landed safe on the other side.
Shrek wandered all night and all the next day
Until the farm and the dogs were far away.
He was safe and free
And on his own
In a mountainous place of rock and stone
Where the air was clear and the water sweet
And there was tussock grass and scrub to eat.
Life now changed for Shrek the wether.
He knew he'd left his friends forever.

Above: Shrek showing children from Ireland the view from his cave in the summer of 2008.

22 Shrek: The story of a Kiwi icon   **Above**: The woolly king with his impenetrable shield.

But he found new friends,
In that place of peace —
Rabbits and birds and a flock of geese.
He watched the seasons come and go.
Summers were hot. Winters brought snow.
Shrek the sheep grew big and strong.
His uncut fleece was thick and long.
He walked the hills
Like a woolly king,
A friend to every living thing.
But when a wild dog dared come there,
Shrek butted and tossed it in the air.
Years went by and Shrek grew old.
He lived in a cave during winter cold.
His steps were shaky
Through rain and snow.
For he no longer saw the way to go.
This big old sheep, so brave and wise
Had grown wool over both his eyes
One day, some musterers came that way
To round up sheep that had gone astray.
Shrek heard the dogs,
He twitched his ears
As he remembered his early fears.
He stood dead still in the midday sun.
He couldn't see and he couldn't run.
Then Ann, a musterer, stopped with a cry:
'Is that a sheep we've just passed by?
'He's humungous!
'A monster! Heck!
'But he's so gentle, we'll call him Shrek!'
Then careful hands picked Shrek up
And put him on the musterers' truck.
Back at the farm, word soon went round,
That a monstrous wether had been found.

J.Chisholm © artist

Crowds came to see,
They stood in queues,
And Shrek appeared on the six o'clock news.
His fame soon spread throughout the land.
No one had seen a fleece so grand.
There were flashing cameras and hearty cheers
As Shrek's great coat went to the shears.
Snip, snip to his tail,
Snip, snip to his neck.
And finally out of the fleece came Shrek.
His eyes were clear. At last he could see.
Shrek the famous sheep was free.
Shrek's way of life on the hills was gone

Above and opposite: Sketches by Jenny Chisholm, who illustrated the best-selling *Shrek: The famous hermit sheep of Tarras.*

But he had a new friend in his owner John.
John takes good care
Of the famous sheep
And the fleece displayed in a mountainous heap.
Shrek and John move from show to show
Raising funds for children wherever they go.
Even the Prime Minister travelled to see
The sheep who is now a celebrity.
His fame has spread
To faraway shores
As he raises funds for a worthy cause.
People call him a miraculous thing.
Yes, Shrek the sheep is still the king.

Chapter 1

Finding Shrek, the Hermit Merino

As two musterers and their dogs drove a mob of 1000 or so merino ewes across the vast alpine tussock land above Bendigo Station, high up on top of a rocky outcrop a huge woolly sheep stood motionless.

Against the backdrop of the endless Central Otago sky, it looked almost god-like, its fleece so massive that even with the binoculars it was hard to make out if it was a sheep or not. There were no legs and no head to be seen — just a huge round mass and a pink nose.

Merinos are normally shorn annually, but this particular animal had clearly been hiding out in caves, avoiding the annual muster for who knows how long. Over the years its unshorn fleece had matted and grown to resemble its environment. Dust had stuck to the lanolin in the wool and bits of matagouri and other plant matter had become stuck in the fibres, creating a perfect camouflage. By standing still it was, presumably, hoping to avoid the detection of the musterers yet again.

On this particular day, 15 April 2004, Ann Scanlan, Daniel Devine ('Cage') and I had left the homestead down on the valley floor below just before daybreak. With winter on the way, the morning had a sharp bite to it as we made the hour-long drive up the very rough four-wheel-drive tracks to the top of Bendigo.

Normally we'd have taken the double-cab Hilux ute with the dog boxes on the back. But it happened to be at the mechanic's this day so we were in the Landcruiser instead, a coincidence that was to work in Shrek's favour. The dogs rode in a trailer on the back.

It was the first of a run of incredible and bizarre coincidences that saved Shrek's life. It is also important to understand that at the time Shrek was found we were not exactly lifestyle farmers. Bendigo Station covered 11,000 hectares (30,000 acres) and was running 18,000 of Shrek's merino cousins, with a further 10,000 being run on neighbouring sister properties Long Gully and Deep Creek.

Left: Icicles form just below the site of Shrek's cave. It is truly amazing that he survived so many winters up there on his own.

Above: Not all merino are renegades. Ann Scanlan hard at work mustering merino wethers.

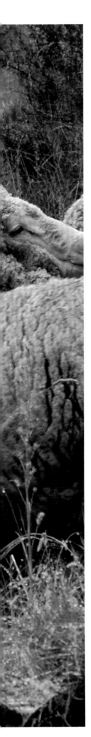

On our partnership properties Otamatapaio and Rugged Ridges in the Waitaki Valley and Holbrook and Glenrock in the Mackenzie, a further 30,000 merino were being run in an international partnership with fine-wool fabric manufacturers, the Lempriere and Botto families from Italy. This gave a total flock of close to 60,000 and the opportunity to foster individual sheep did not exist. In fact the law of nature and survival transformed the merino into a very hardy breed requiring little to no individual attention. We certainly had no time to hide a pet lamb on the top of Bendigo as has been a common theory from across the Tasman.

The mob was spread out over about 800 hectares so I dropped Ann and Cage at different points to start their beats. Ann is an exceptionally skilled musterer but spends a lot of time in an office managing three high country stations, so when I had phoned offering her a day's work bringing the ewes off the summer country, she had jumped at the chance. A casual musterer, Cage was less experienced but was still pretty good too, and so on this particular day the muster went well with the ewes arriving at the gate within an hour or so.

Quietness gradually descended again on the lone woolly's alpine paradise. Way below came the sound of the odd 'baa' as the mob of ewes spread out, grazing new pasture far

It was unusual for a hermit woolly to come out in the open like that as they would normally do their best to hide out in the rocks.

below. In a few hours the overgrown sheep would be totally alone except for the rabbits, and the occasional native hawk soaring the sky.

It was unusual for a hermit woolly to come out in the open like that as they would normally do their best to hide out in the rocks. There were 150-metre vertical bluffs falling away to each side and it was incredible that he had managed to climb to this point, carrying what we later learnt was more than his body weight in wool.

I have often wondered why he chose to come out of hiding on that day? It was the first time in five years that there had been ewes in that top block so perhaps he had caught a whiff of them. Or maybe he was hungry and knew he wouldn't survive if he stayed another winter up there.

Unbeknown to the woolly, Ann had been watching it. She tells me all had been going well, with the ewes stringing along her beat, but when she'd looked behind to see if any sheep had been missed she'd spotted this large object. It was quite

Above: Although they might make for impressive photos, winters at Bendigo can be harsh, as seen through the window of this iconic miners' cottage in Welshtown.

some distance away so she couldn't fathom what it was but it was very gradually moving along, trying to keep up with the ewes.

She knew it would make her late but she went back to get a better view of this thing, climbing up and dropping back behind just in case it got her scent. To her amazement, it was the biggest woolly she had ever seen.

This woolly was trying its best to walk along the narrow sheep track but was struggling because it couldn't see anything with that amount of wool over its eyes. Every now and then it would stop and lift its head up so the wool would fall back and it could see. Then away it would go again. It finally got down to the end of the sheep track. It had a couple of little streams to cross then a tussock face to climb. With all the wool it was carrying, Ann thought there was no way it could manage the climb.

Ann was well off my beat by this time and her mob of ewes were a long way ahead so she decided to leave it there. As she swung around and climbed up on top to catch up with her mob we met up, and I was looking at her as if to say, 'What have you been doing all this time, Ann?'

Ann proceeded to explain that she had seen the biggest woolly ever and that he was coming up behind her. I replied that we didn't have time to be hanging around waiting for a tardy woolly.

Once we hooked the head and headed them back towards the gate, however, we swung around to see if this woolly had climbed on to the top. Sure enough, there was this big woolly, trying to see where the mob had gone.

'To make sure you get him you'll have to get underneath and come up,' I said to Ann.

So off she went with her dogs, dropping down into the bluffs the woolly had climbed through. Very cautiously, Ann climbed up behind and into a position where the woolly wouldn't get the scent of her or her dogs. Once in a good position, she told her dogs to stay back at the bluffs and then she very quietly stalked the woolly until she knew she could run him down without him bolting over the bluffs.

It was a daring move, even for this ultra-fit five-foot-something musterer, but with the mountain breeze quietly blowing in the woolly's face, it hadn't been able to hear or smell Ann. When she reached him, Ann rolled him on his back; the heavily laden woolly was going nowhere. Ann kept a strong grip on him until Cage and I approached, which is just as well as he started to panic. We quickly determined the woolly was an old wether and all agreed he was very unusual. After all our years mustering in the high country, none of us had ever seen anything like it. The woolly had at least a foot of wool on him, which meant he had probably been out there for at least five years. The wool on his shoulders was so hard it was like a shield. Merinos are bred to have relatively clean faces but having not been shorn for so long, wool had grown over the wether's eyes, making him wool blind. His pink nose was raw from using it like a blind man's cane to find his way through the rocks and speargrass.

So it was no surprise when Cage said in a deep unemotional voice, 'Do you want me to get a rock and knock it on the head for dog tucker?' A real animal lover, Ann quickly retorted 'No.'

The sheep's fate hung in the balance. Would female compassion win out? He probably wouldn't have survived another winter alone on the tops. It was 10 kilometres back to the station homestead and he certainly couldn't walk that distance.

If we'd had the Hilux as usual there would have been no way to transport the woolly back to the homestead. But since we happened to have the Cruiser, Cage suggested we fold down the back seats and squeeze him in there. Unlike town folk, New Zealand farmers do not generally transport animals inside their vehicles, but this was the only way to get him back to the homestead, so I walked down to the gate to the Cruiser and brought it back up to collect the wether. Laden down with wool, he wasn't able to put up much resistance as he was lifted, pushed and shoved into the back.

Arriving back at the homestead I decided to put the woolly in the ram shed.

Above: There are a lot of places to hide in the Devil's Creek high country if you are a renegade.

Finding Shrek, the Hermit Merino **33**

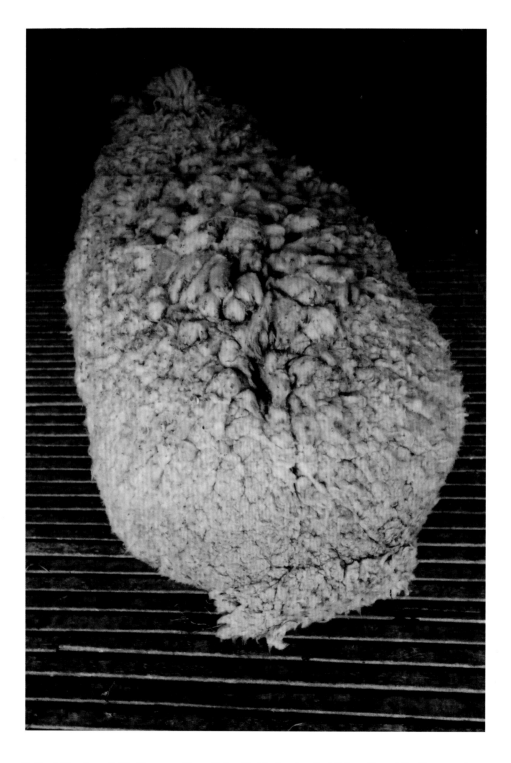

34 Shrek: The story of a Kiwi icon

Above: Before the big shearing, Paul Holmes likened Shrek's rear end to Queen Victoria's gown. In reality, this was the protective layer Shrek needed to survive for so long on his own.

A couple of minutes' walk from the house, the ram shed had been purpose-built a few years earlier to house and display Bendigo's prize merino pedigree stud sheep. It was used for the annual on-farm stud sale and leading up to A&P Shows, but it was empty at the time.

After all those years in the wide-open high country, the woolly bumped around the walls, his only thought finding a way out of the confined space. Being virtually totally wool blind he had no chance, but even so his instinct told him to keep trying.

It wasn't long before a truck pulled up in front of the shed and a group of teenagers asked where they could put their horses and saddles. It was the Hawke's Bay Pony Club team. They were staying at Bendigo for the week and would be competing in the New Zealand champs being held nearby. They needed somewhere to put their saddles so I told them to use the ram shed but warned them to be careful because there was a big woolly bumping about inside.

It was a worthless old woolly and an embarrassment to any self-respecting musterer. Little did we know that this pretty ordinary hermit merino wether was about to hit the big time.

The young riders were fascinated by the woolly and stood leaning on the rail watching him for ages. I explained how Ann had found him earlier that day. Then for some reason I asked the girls, 'Do you think we should give the woolly a name?'

One girl said the woolly looked like an ogre. After a long pause, another girl, Clare Hutchinson, said, 'Why not call it Shrek?'

The animated fairytale movie was popular at the time, although I had never heard of it. Privately I wasn't very impressed with the name but later over a cup of tea Ann and Cage said they thought it was a good idea. What did it really matter anyway? It was a worthless old woolly and an embarrassment to any self-respecting musterer. Little did we know that this pretty ordinary hermit merino wether was about to hit the big time.

The Child Who Loved Animals

Ann Scanlan's story

I believe farming was my destiny. Born on a farm in Milton in South Otago, my life has always been surrounded with animals. I drove my mother and father mad with my assortment of pets — cats, calves, lambs, pups and ponies.

In the early stages of my childhood, my father was a dairy farmer so I had numerous pet calves that grew into dairy cows, all proudly named. I distinctly remember going to my Catholic primary school one winter morning extremely upset. The nun asked me what was wrong so I began to tell her my pet cow Bernadette had died of mastitis the day before. I was inconsolable. As she listened to my sobbing story, to my amazement she made the comment, 'Well, Ann, she was only a cow.' As a child who loved animals this was not the comment or comfort I was looking for from my teacher.

I used to dream of having a team of dogs and mustering sheep with a horse. I used to get into terrible trouble with my father John when I would secretly take his dogs down to the paddock to chase the sheep and caused some major mess-ups.

In the last year of school we went on a trip through the Lindis Pass. When we stopped at the top of the pass, I was blown away by the scenery, the tussocks, the vastness and the ambience. This was me. I decided to leave school and work as a farm cadet so eventually I'd end up in the high country.

In the late 1980s I spent some time working in the North Island shepherding on Tautane Station for manager Bob Bryson. The grounding and experience

I gained during my time there was invaluable. At Tautane we all used to have a lambing beat. The property was running 21,000 breeding ewes so, with four shepherds, we would each end up with 4000 to 5000 ewes on our lambing beats.

Some shepherds would be home by lunchtime or mid-afternoon. But because I am a great believer that where there is life there is hope, some days I would end up riding home in the dark.

When I secured a job managing Otamatapaio Station in the Waitaki Valley near Lake Benmore, I quickly accumulated a family of pets — Fred and Charlie the orphan calves, Smoke the fallow deer and Lucy the lamb, six ducks from Wongs at Tarras that grew into a family of 17 ducks. They all seemed to arrive about the same time and were great friends, cruising around the drive at Otamatapaio like they owned the place.

Smoke the fallow deer thought he was a cat. From a very early age he would come inside and jump on my knee and sit there. But Smoke grew quickly and was soon too big for this kind of carry on! He also loved running through the house on the carpet and jumping all over the furniture. Fortunately, fallow deer are very sensitive on their feet so there were no major breakages or accidents.

Above: Ann relaxing in front of her television with Smoke the fallow deer.

The last cup of tea at Birchwood, with several generations of the Williamson family. In 2004, Birchwood Station was purchased by the government's Nature Heritage Fund.

As the adults discuss politics and heritage, Shrek entertains the younger Williamsons.

Birchwood Station was part of government plans for a network of South Island high country reserves, for both conservation and recreational purposes.

Careful, Shrek!

No harm done!

The Life of Shrek
Visiting Birchwood

Above: Centuries of blizzards carved these rocks, that stand majestically over Bendigo Station, and created the cave that became Shrek's hideaway for five years.

Above: Even when he was wool blind Shrek carried with him an air of importance.

Chapter 2

Overnight Celebrity

As the pony club riders left the shed, the Bendigo gamekeeper Steve Brown turned up to see what was so interesting. He was good friends with Stephen Jaquiery, an award-winning photographer at the *Otago Daily Times* newspaper based three hours away in Dunedin.

'Do you think Stephen would like to take a photo of Shrek for the paper?' I asked.

Stephen had met Steve when trying to catch Slippery Jack, a trophy stag which had saved its own neck by escaping from Bendigo's game park and was upsetting the Tarras community by running amok, creating havoc in people's gardens and the like.

Stephen was in bed having a lie-in at his parents' house in Wanaka when the telephone call came.

'Gidday, Steve Brown speaking. I wonder if you want to come through to Bendigo and photograph a sheep with a large fleece?'

'What? Why would I want to do that?'

Long before that day, one of the things Stephen had decided was that, although he was never going to be rolling rich being a newspaper photographer, he could be rich in experiences and with the friends he met through the job. He liked Steve Brown. He trusted his judgement, and even if the sheep turned out to be a fizzer he guessed they might go and shoot a rabbit or a pheasant, or even a deer.

When Stephen arrived he was less than impressed with what he saw. The woolly in the ram shed just looked like a great scruffy ball of wool. How could he possibly get a great shot of that? Perhaps it would look more impressive with a better background.

'Okay,' said Stephen. 'Let's take him up onto the rocks behind the ram shed.' He was referring to rocky outcrops similar, although much smaller, than those where Shrek had been found. They could be accessed by four-wheel-drive motorbike,

Above: The photo that took the world by storm, making Shrek a media sensation overnight. It was the beginning of a great journey that continues to raise funds for Cure Kids, an organisation helping children all across New Zealand.

so I suggested putting the small stock trailer on the back to get Shrek up there.

Being wool blind, Shrek didn't have a clue what was happening when Cage pulled him out of the ram shed. A big raw-boned southern man, Cage had plenty of experience moving unwilling subjects about from his part-time job as a bouncer at the local Shooters Bar in Wanaka. Another person who had happy memories of holidays at Bendigo as a youngster, Cage was a bit of a rough diamond and had been given the nickname Cagefighter as a result of his exploits while working at nearby Cluden Station, but really he had a heart of gold.

Up on the rocky outcrop, Stephen took a few photos of me crouching next to Shrek, while the others looked on. Stephen was underwhelmed and within a few minutes the photo shoot was over. 'That's all I can do,' he said as he started putting his camera away.

Digger, the gamekeeper's assistant, had been watching the whole time. He was a stout little chap and Cage was always reminding him that he was a little runt. But they were the best of mates and often went out hunting together on the wild West Coast or up some mountain somewhere.

With the photo shoot over, I told Cage to put Shrek back in the trailer parked about 10 metres away. Watching Cage push the unwilling sheep across towards the trailer, Digger said, 'I bet you can't carry that thing over your shoulders, Cage.' Cage fancied himself as a bit of a strongman so took the bait and bent over to pick up Shrek and hoist him around his shoulders. After all the years of not being able to look after his private parts, Shrek wasn't pretty underneath but Cage didn't smell that good himself after a night out at the Shooters Bar.

Otago Daily Times

Telephone (03) 477-4760   THURSDAY, April 29, 2004   80c (75c delivered) North Isl. air freight 30c extra

un in the sun	**Festival shaping up**		**New motoring**
Kiwi's date with .oos tabloid fodder	Arts feast for city in October	MODEL EXAMPLE	**magazine**
General **3**	Dunedin **5**		Inside tomorrow

Wily old wether transformed into stage performer

World stops as Shrek fleeced

By Dave Cannan

Bendigo: A man shore a sheep in Cromwell last night and the whole world watched.

Yes, it does sound like make-believe, but then, there has been something surreal about the story of Shrek, the hermit merino, and his return from six years in the wilderness ever since he hit the front page of the *Otago Daily Times* almost two weeks ago.

The fairytale continued in the conference room of the Golden Gate Hotel in Cromwell last night as television crews beamed images around the world of Omarama shearer Peter Casserly gently removing the 9-year-old's monster fleece with super-sharp blades.

Who could believe such an event would attract so much media attention; that major news networks such as CNN, BBC, Reuters, Channels 7, 9 and 10 in Australia, and APTN in Hong Kong would take live feeds from the *Holmes* show; that print media from around New Zealand would hungrily devour words and photographs of the

de-fleecing of a nondescript sheep from the heart of Central Otago?

No-one, including the media themselves; that's who. Broadcaster Paul Holmes told the *ODT* last night he believed Shrek was responsible for his own celebrity status.

"He's a star; that's why," he said. "I met him today and was quite taken with him.

"You only have to watch him walk along behind [owner] John Perriam like a dog to see that. He has a presence; he's so placid, considering he's been out in the hills for so long on his own."

In other words, there is nothing nondescript about Shrek. The sheep has style; a sense of occasion. And it's true: he follows Mr Perriam around like a well-trained and dutiful pet.

After being transported from Bendigo Station to Cromwell last night, Shrek followed his master through the gates of the hotel, across a courtyard through a milling crowd, and waited to be hoisted into a holding pen.

Then, when it was time for the grand entrance into the conference room ablaze with lights and a noisy, 200-plus strong crowd, Shrek made another dutiful walk, was lifted

on to the stage and stood quietly in front of the cameras without turning so much as a staple of his shaggy fleece.

The transformation of Shrek from a musterer-shy loner into a sheep of the world puzzled many onlookers, but big Dan Devine, the strapping musterer who has carried the sheep across his shoulders, says it is all about friendship.

"John has been hand-feeding him since we found him and he's responded to that. I suppose Shrek's been up in the

hills looking for a friend for the last six years and now he's found one."

Mr Perriam admits he is quite taken with the wether and, as the sheep's fame has spread like wildfire around the world, especially with children, he has become increasingly concerned about Shrek's welfare.

That is why early yesterday, on a bitterly cold Central Otago morning, he decided Shrek needed to be shorn with blades, rather than a machine,

to ensure a generous layer of wool remained on him.

And that is also why last night, after all the fuss was over, Mr Perriam took Shrek back to Bendigo Station and put him in a heated room, even though the sheep was wearing a specially-made, triple-layer, merino-wool Icebreaker cover.

Continued on page 2

● Shrek 'wannabes'   — p2

Top: Two woolly heads . . . *Holmes* television show presenter Paul Holmes head to head with Shrek, and the sheep's owner, John Perriam, during Holmes' live broadcast from the Golden Gate Hotel in Cromwell. Above: Shrek or Shaun? . . . Shrek, minus his own coat of six years, but plus his specially-made Icebreaker merino-wool coat, with Mr Perriam.

PHOTOS: STEPHEN JAQUIERY

Fleeced in front of a crowd . . . World blade-shearing champion Peter Casserly takes a break from his hefty task, as Shrek, the merino, lies on his 20.5kg fleece in Cromwell last night. They are watched by world champion machine shearer David Fagan (centre, standing on stage).

2 men arrested with NZ passport fakes

Wellington: New Zealand embassy officials in Bangkok were investigating reports yesterday of 11 fake New Zealand passports with possible al Qaeda links being found by Thai police on Monday.

The discovery of the documents followed the detention a month ago of a Pakistan national who, when arrested, was found with a dozen fake New Zealand passports, the *Bangkok Post* newspaper reported.

On Monday night, Thai police arrested a Thai man and a Pakistani man for allegedly producing forged passports which might have been used by al Qaeda-linked terrorist suspects arrested in Europe, the newspaper said.

The two men were arrested with 23 fake passports, including "11 fake passports being passed off as New Zealand documents and 10 as French".

The two men, named as Decha Kaeoprakhong (31) and Mohammad Iqbal (36), were arrested in an area of Bangkok frequented by overseas Muslims visiting Thailand.

All the passports bore serial numbers starting with key numbers that enabled the holder to travel to many countries without requiring a visa.

Crime Suppression Division Commander, Kosin Hinthao, told reporters New Zealand police had identified the passport identification numbers as similar to those used by human traffickers and al Qaeda terrorists in Europe.

"Many terrorists arrested earlier in Europe had travelled to several nations carrying fake passports with such serial numbers," Mr Kosin said.

Ministry of Foreign Affairs and Trade media adviser Jonathan Schwass told NZPA yesterday this country's embassy in Bangkok was aware of the story.

Mike Bush, a police officer attached to the embassy, had been involved in dealing with the matter.

Mr Schwass said he was unsure how accurate the news paper report was.

The office of Internal Affairs Minister George Hawkins whose department issues passports, said Mr Hawkins was aware of the report.

Above: Suddenly Shrek was front page news. How quickly things had changed — for five years, no one knew he even existed.

The pony club girls were right. Draped around Cage's shoulders like a giant shawl, Shrek did look like a monster. Stephen, with the X-factor in photography, was desperately trying to get his camera out of his bag before Cage dropped Shrek back onto the trailer. He only managed

The international news agency Reuters pushed the button and, within 24 hours, the photo of Cage and Shrek had been published in newspapers and on websites all over the world.

to get one shot but later, back in the farm office looking over the photos, we agreed it was the one that clearly stood out from the rest.

'I think we'll send this one down and see what the editor does with it,' Stephen said.

Little did we know, but the acting chief reporter was totally unimpressed with the photo. She was about to discard it when someone walking by asked: 'What the hell is that?'

The *Otago Daily Times* published the photo on its front page, and all the other major New Zealand newspapers followed suit. Then the international news

Above: From the moment Shrek's photo appeared in the Otago Daily Times, my cellphone rang constantly. It seemed everyone wanted to know his story. The appetite and power of the media was extraordinary as it was a feel-good story, rather than an accident, a murder or a war.

Overnight Celebrity **47**

agency Reuters pushed the button and, within 24 hours, the photo of Cage and Shrek had been published in newspapers and on websites all over the world. The world loved the story about the hermit merino sheep being found on the top of Bendigo after successfully evading musterers for five years. Shrek was an instant sensation.

Trying to run the station became impossible because my cellphone rang constantly. Journalists from all over the world wanted to know more about this giant woolly sheep. Where was he found? What did he live on? How did you catch him? The list of questions went on and on.

In those first few days after capture, everyone wanted their photo taken with Shrek. My experience showing sheep for judges was invaluable as Shrek was constantly moved to stand in the right place for the camera. To everyone's amazement, this sheep that just days ago was living wild up in his hermit's cave responded calmly — although when he got tired he would just sit down.

Most New Zealand farmers have little experience dealing with the media and would have been completely overwhelmed with the media frenzy. But, as luck would have it, I was well aware of how the media ticked after many years involved in farming politics. TV crews started turning up unannounced and it became a full-time job trying to negotiate them — each channel trying to get a new and exclusive angle on Shrek's story.

A large number of local radio stations and newspapers turned up too. Overseas

Above: Cage became a bit of an overnight celebrity himself. Here he took the opportunity with Holmes to let the world know he was single and fancied Canadian girls.

media outlets such as CNN, BBC and Channel 9 in Australia added to the constant barrage. The media even started reporting on the incredible amount of international media attention Shrek was attracting.

New Zealand farmers and everyone at Bendigo shook our heads in amazement. Why was there all this interest in Shrek? He was just a sheep and New Zealand had over 30 million of them. All he had done was avoid the annual autumn muster. But people love a story of animal survival and outsmarting humans. The world was tired of all the gruesome war coverage of Iraq and wanted to feel good for a change.

It is difficult to put into words the pressure the media put us under and I was determined not to allow a good story to become derailed by one bad media report as could so easily happen.

Two key elements that gave absolute credibility to the Shrek story were that Cage and Ann were there when he was found and during the days that followed and that I was the sole spokesman, with no committees or board to contend with.

I realised every decision was critical in the eye of the public and media. I was fully aware we had been handed a very special gift and it was up to me to make the most of the opportunity in every way possible.

Meanwhile, Shrek was rapidly developing a close bond with me. He felt secure around me and would come up to me, even when he was still wool blind, to sniff my hand. With a strong sense of smell, he could pick me out from a large group of people just as ewes can pick their lambs out of hundreds within minutes. It is a unique attribute sheep have as animals. Just imagine blindfolding 100 human mothers and their children. What chaos!

Moving Shrek from the high tops to the confinement of the ram shed at Bendigo was a radical change of environment and diet. I felt a great responsibility to do the right thing. Shrek had lived on a wholly organic diet for years — pure alpine water, native herbs and grasses and blue tussock.

From years of feeding pedigree show sheep, I knew how to manage the transition. To bring him down and put him in a highly fertilised grass paddock would have been disaster without a high level of roughage to balance his diet. Merinos are browsing animals and love a diet of low-nutritional plants found in the high country of New Zealand and the most important thing, as for humans, is that they have a balanced diet. Even feeding him on high-octane barley, wheat or other mixes would have seen Shrek's journey shortlived. We knew from experience he needed to stay on a low-protein diet and not have a radical change to his metabolism.

With Shrek's story running hotter than ever in the media, local people and farmers started to say the whole bizarre story was a jack-up. How could an old wether survive alone up in the mountains all those years? It just wasn't possible. And why was he so tame? Perhaps he'd been a pet lamb that had lost its normal mob instinct?

I could see why farmers were sceptical. It was highly unlikely that a sheep could evade musterers for five years and survive at 1400 metres through intense

heat and deep snow. Yes, Shrek was unusually sociable but no, he had not been a pet lamb. Sometimes truth can be stranger than fiction.

Heather and I were blown away by the level of media interest but we felt very isolated and wondered how we could use it for good. Bendigo had already hosted a mystery weekend for Cure Kids — an organisation that raises funds for child health research and that already had many famous human ambassadors, including All Black greats Jonah Lomu and Anton Oliver. So I rang the CEO, Kaye Parker, in Queenstown and asked, 'Would Cure Kids like a famous sheep too?'

While Cure Kids was well known in the corporate world, the public awareness was limited because the brand was only four years old. Shrek coming on board

Above: Shrek's daily ration of chaff and white oats — the high fibre, low protein diet that has helped him to live to be the oldest sheep living in New Zealand today.

as a celebrity ambassador would change everything. Suddenly Cure Kids would be the most talked-about charity in the country. No one knew how big the Shrek opportunity was going to be but that wasn't surprising. There had never been anything like it in New Zealand.

'Yes, we would be honoured to be Shrek's charity of choice,' said Kaye.

From the moment we decided to use Shrek to promote Cure Kids, the whole country, including the doubters, got right in behind the woolly hermit from Bendigo. Cure Kids contacted Dreamworks, the owners of the Shrek brand, which generously agreed to let the woolly sheep from a tiny country called New Zealand keep his multimillion-dollar brand name if it helped sick children.

An amazing career was about to unfold — but first there was the matter of removing all that wool!

Above: This cartoon, by Allan Hawkey, was first featured in the *Waikato Times*.

Above: A typical winter scene in Central Otago, hoar frost in the Ida Valley near Oturehua.

The friendly staff of BNZ Cromwell.

'Look at the camera, Shrek!' say these boys on the beaches of St Kilda, Dunedin.

With no lead, Shrek marches into Alexandra Library and mingles with the children.

On tour in the Super City, outside Auckland War Memorial Museum.

Shrek stands with incredible presence, alongside the Chittick family of Waikato Stud.

The Life of Shrek

Meeting new friends

Above: 'What's going on here, John?' Shrek wondering what all the fuss is about, before his first shearing and after becoming a star.

Chapter 3

The Big Shearing

The week after Shrek was found, the National Pony Club Champs were held at the Cromwell racecourse, but they received very little attention from the media. Shrek was still the big news story of the day.

Animal welfare activists started writing to papers saying Shrek was suffering, carrying around all that wool. He should be shorn immediately. Failure to do so was sending a bad signal to all farmers about how to treat their animals.

According to the official farming code of practice, sheep should be shorn once a year and at the right time to minimise stress on the animal. But as the world was discovering, Shrek wasn't excited by the rules or proper conduct of a sheep.

The National Champs hierarchy hatched a cunning plan that Shrek should be shorn in front of 300 young riders at the grand dinner to be held in the Bendigo woolshed on the conclusion of the champs. By now my family had had enough of the media attention and thought the shearing was a good idea. Without his wool, Shrek would just be an ordinary old wether again, right?

But the day of the dinner — when Cage, Ann and I were at the homestead for yet another TV interview — we all expressed discomfort about Shrek being put on display and shorn that night. It was uncanny that all three of us agreed, so I made the decision not to shear him.

Heather and the pony club hierarchy were very disappointed but I stuck to my guns, even though I couldn't justify my decision. The grand dinner still took place 200 metres away from Shrek's shed. Everybody still had a great time — the area between Shrek's shed and the woolshed resembled a New Year's Eve downtown in Wanaka with groups of kids sitting in huddles or wandering around.

Into the early hours of the morning, Shrek had a continual stream of young visitors. Someone had the bright idea of pegging back the wool that had been hanging over Shrek's eyes so he could see the teenagers sneaking a drink of alcohol and lighting up fags when the authorities and parents couldn't see them in the dark. Shrek had a great time that night. Clearly he wasn't the only rebel in the world.

The next morning my cellphone went off yet again.

'Gidday mate, Paul Holmes here from TV One. They tell me you have a big woolly. How would you like to shear him in front of the world?'

Paul Holmes was the host of his own current affairs TV show, the *Holmes* show, which was watched by hundreds of thousands of New Zealanders every night after their dinner. By now I was used to getting calls from the media but I was staggered when Holmes said the footage would be used by CNN. That meant worldwide coverage! Managing the Shrek phenomenon was turning out to be like trying to ride a runaway racehorse.

We had been so close to shearing Shrek the night before at the pony club dinner, and now we had the media opportunity of a lifetime. This kind of exposure would be massive for New Zealand, Central Otago, Cure Kids and the New Zealand merino industry. It was the sort of profile money simply couldn't buy.

I tried to explain to Paul that shearing Shrek on live TV was a very risky thing

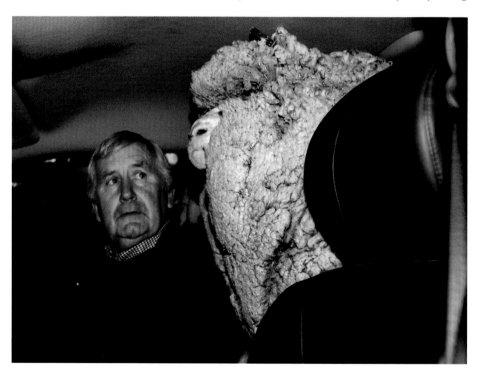

Above: Shrek and I on our way to the big shearing at the Golden Gate Lodge, Cromwell. I was very nervous before the event, but Shrek stayed calm the whole time. It turned out he was a natural in front of the cameras.

to do. If Shrek's skin was cut or he couldn't stand up after being relieved of all that wool it could ruin New Zealand's animal welfare reputation overnight. But I quickly found Holmes, like Shrek, had a mind of his own.

'Don't worry. I have New Zealand champion shearer Dave Fagan ready to go,' said Holmes.

I said, 'Okay, I'll think about it, Paul.' But feeling the pressure, I soon rang back. The date was set for a week's time.

To let the Central Otago locals meet Shrek, we decided to hold an open day at Bendigo. Thousands of people turned up, as well as TV One journalists and other media. It was a beautiful day and there were queues of people waiting to get their photo taken with Shrek. There was a haybale-throwing contest and Cage did a strongman demonstration, carrying a 200-kilogram bale of wool on his back. Willy Wong, a neighbour and bit of hermit himself, brought his kunekune pigs along so the kids could play catch the greasy pig. Unfortunately, Willy used oil rather than grease and the kids got into a hell of a mess.

Holmes wanted the shearing to take place at Bendigo, so a team of technicians came down from Wellington and climbed up trees and onto the roofs of sheds,

Above: An excited crowd, and world, wait in anticipation for the event.   The Big Shearing **59**

trying to get a signal to beam live to the world. Unfortunately broadband was not available in the back country back then, and so Holmes had to settle on the event being held at the Golden Gate Lodge at Cromwell, 10 minutes' drive away. Needless to say, broadband was put into Bendigo the month after Shrek was shorn.

As the day drew closer, I started to think about how to raise as much money as possible from the televised shearing. That's when we came up with the idea of creating limited-edition souvenirs of Shrek's wool. Staples of his wool would be contained in display boxes along with the Shrek story and a numbered

certificate of authenticity signed by me and Shrek's shearer David Fagan.

With only 10 days until the shearing, we set to work cold-calling to find a company to make the boxes. It was a real setback when the first 100 boxes arrived and we found they were only 15 centimetres long. Shrek's fleece was 33 centimetres and there was no way I would allow it to be folded in half! New boxes were quickly made but for many nights it was all hands on deck compiling the boxed sets.

The outdoor clothing company Icebreaker agreed to make five tops out of some of Shrek's fleece. Two would be auctioned — one online and the other

Above: 'Paul, look at me! It's not all about you, you know.'

one at a later event. The remaining three tops would be given to New Zealand mountaineering legend Sir Edmund Hillary, Prime Minister Helen Clark and Andrew Adamson, the Kiwi director of the *Shrek* movies.

Telecom offered to provide a free 09004SHREK phone number so viewers could ring to automatically make donations to Cure Kids. I wanted Holmes to run the phone number along the bottom of the screen during the shearing but he wasn't having a bar of it, saying, 'I'm not a bloody charity.'

I knew I needed to keep feeding the news

We knew the only way Shrek would have survived the deep midwinter snow would have been by living among the north-facing overhanging rocks that faced the sun.

media to maintain their interest in Shrek because the shearing was still several days away. I wracked my brains for what else I could possibly tell them about a simple sheep. That's when Ann, Steve the gamekeeper and I decided to go back up to where Shrek was found and see if we could find anything of interest.

We knew the only way Shrek would have survived the deep midwinter snow would have been by living among the north-facing overhanging rocks that faced the sun. We spent hours looking around and found several little streams of alpine water running close by and small pools of water among

Above: Peter Casserly shears Shrek while world champion David Fagan watches on.   The Big Shearing **61**
What a great job Peter did at a moment's notice under the pressure of live TV.
And with only one small dram.

62 Shrek: The story of a Kiwi icon

Above: Jimmy Barnett lends a hand as Peter shears Shrek. Jimmy was later to shear Shrek on an iceberg off the coast of New Zealand. David Fagan and Cage watch on. Far right is Paul Holmes in full cry.

the speargrass and native flora between the rock outcrops. The only signs of life were hawks and magpies overhead and the odd hare.

The tranquillity and magic views from this little mountain paradise were amazing, but after a time we decided there was nothing of real significance that might interest the media. We started to walk back up a dark face covered in speargrass, directly below where Ann had caught Shrek. Halfway up we ducked behind a larger group of rocks.

'I think I've found Shrek's cave,' I said.

Out the front was the majestic view of the Upper Clutha Valley and the Pisa Range covered with snow, with the sun starting to set on the golden tussocks. It was the perfect window onto a pristine view of New Zealand. As it was on the dark south-facing side of the hill, Shrek would have used it for shade in the summer.

I went down the hill very excited with my find as I knew the media were hungry for more stories. Back at the homestead I rang TV One and within an hour I took a call from the *Holmes* show.

'They tell me you've found Shrek's cave,' Paul said. 'I want exclusive coverage.'

'I want you to run the 09004SHREK for Cure Kids during the shearing, Paul.'

We had a deal!

The day of the shearing, I was up before daylight to feed Shrek and take the dogs for a walk. It was a cold frosty autumn morning and a chilly breeze was blowing up from the south.

The night before I had lain awake worrying. What if Shrek got cut by the shearing comb? What if Shrek couldn't walk after he was shorn? There was so much that could go wrong in full view of the world. It was one of the biggest risks I'd ever taken.

Walking along the frozen ground, I continued to mull over the situation. Holmes had arranged for the world's number-one machine-shearer, Kiwi David Fagan, to shear Shrek. He was staying in Cromwell and was ready to go. Paul Holmes was to arrive at midday with sidekick Brent Fraser.

Although the live show was only hours away, I decided it was too big a risk to shear Shrek with a machine-driven handpiece. Instead he would be shorn the traditional way by hand with blade shears. Like a giant pair of scissors, blades leave more wool on the sheep to keep the animal warm and, for this reason, are still used today on many of New Zealand's more snow-prone high country stations.

He realised I was not just a simple 'tussock jumper' who could be pushed around even by the number-one media frontman in New Zealand.

Back at the homestead I rang Holmes in Wellington and told him my decision. Paul swore and shouted in a way that would have impressed the most hardened musterer. But all to no avail. He realised I was not just a simple 'tussock jumper' who could be pushed around even by the number-one media frontman in New Zealand.

Paul couldn't or wouldn't understand my reasoning — although, not being a farmer, that was hardly surprising.

'Do you realise I have paid for David to fly down?'

'Yes,' I said. 'He will be our ambassador during the shearing. He is a world champion.'

'Well, who the hell have you got with a set of blades that can shear Shrek?'

'Peter Casserly,' I said.

'Never heard of him,' Holmes said.

'He's a New Zealand champion blade shearer,' I said.

'Right. I'll see you at midday, mate,' Paul said.

In fact, I had not at that stage even spoken to Peter Casserly, so as I hung up the phone from Holmes, I was frantically looking up the Omarama phone directory for Peter's number. It was only 12 hours before the shearing was due to take place in front of the world. He'd better be home!

'Would you mind shearing a big woolly for me today, Peter?' I said.

'No worries,' replied Peter.

Peter hadn't been following the news and he didn't realise he would be doing it in front of 1.2 billion viewers! Just a minor detail.

At midday a Squirrel helicopter arrived to fly the *Holmes* crew up to pre-record an exclusive visit to Shrek's cave. Brent Fraser had arrived, but where was Paul Holmes? Time was rolling on. Then I got a call from the little village at Tarras, population eight. Paul was just 10 minutes down the road but he was lost!

Eventually he turned up, wearing brand new smooth-soled RM Williams riding boots. I said, 'You'd better swap them for something more practical,' as they would be slippery walking down the hill to the cave. But no dice. Paul felt good in them on flat ground. They wouldn't be a problem on the hill, said the boy from the city.

To strains of *The Sound of Music* we flew south to Devil's Creek, then up the massive rocky canyon towards Castle Rock, high up above Bendigo.

Above: Tom Scott captured the moment beautifully. This cartoon was first published in the *Dominion Post*.

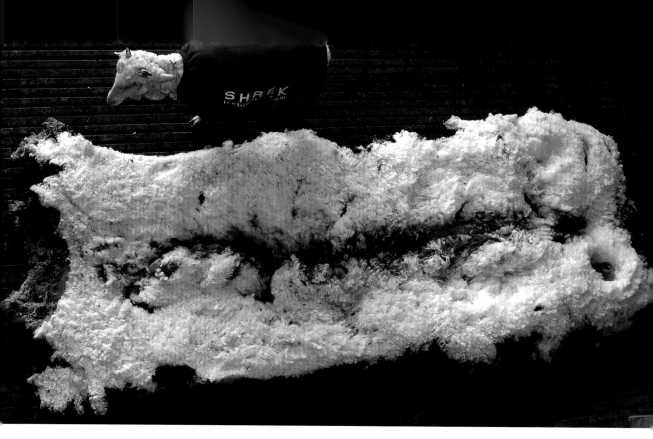

'There's the cave,' said Ann. And down the chopper went, landing directly above where Ann had caught Shrek.

I had quite a job getting Paul down to the cave in his slippery riding boots. I was ready to catch him if he fell but knew New Zealanders would never forgive me if I saved this city slicker from getting a little scratched up in the prickly speargrass. Paul managed to stay on his feet and the amazing views Shrek privately enjoyed were the envy of the world when they were televised prior to the shearing later that day.

Back at the station the excitement was building, with the *Holmes* team trying to keep other media away. Eventually it was time to go to the Golden Gate Lodge for the big event. Cage, all dressed up in his big black cowboy hat, and I jumped in the front of the Jeep and put Shrek in the back to look out the window. To our amazement, paparazzi had parked outside the gate at Bendigo and were now in hot pursuit, driving alongside as they tried to photograph Shrek inside.

The Golden Gate management was outstanding, allowing film crews unlimited access to organise their broadcasts, and Cure Kids took over the restaurant to host their guests. It was definitely not business as usual that night, but nothing

Above: Shrek stands beside his massive 27-kilogram fleece in his new Icebreaker cover. It's hard to imagine how different he must have felt after shedding all that weight. It is incredible he carried this fleece for so long in treacherous mountain conditions.

was a problem as far as the management was concerned.

When we arrived just on nightfall, it was as if a rock star had turned up at the Oscars. Flashing lights were going off everywhere and the place was absolutely packed. Much to my relief, Shrek wasn't at all worried by all the attention and calmly followed me through the gates of the hotel, across a courtyard to make his grand entrance into the conference room, ablaze with lights and packed with a noisy crowd of over 200 people. Shrek was lifted onto the stage to join Peter Casserly, David Fagan, Cage, Paul Holmes and me.

Meanwhile, the *Holmes* team tried to keep all other media out, but were overpowered and there was a real media scrum as reporters pushed and shoved for position. A TV3 reporter fell over and injured her leg; I noticed she had it braced the following morning.

Holmes was in full cry by this time, however, and, as several cartoonists later pointed out, he was clearly enjoying the fact that the world was watching him and seemed for a moment to forget that the world wanted to see Shrek, not him.

Above: This cartoon by Garrick Tremain first featured in *The Press*.   The Big Shearing **67**

Shrek stood calmly on the stage in front of the cameras and when I rolled him over to be shorn, he lay there unrestrained with all four legs sticking up in the air, to the gasps of the crowd. This was a move Shrek and I had practised many times at Bendigo. When Peter Casserly picked up his blades and started to remove Shrek's huge fleece, Holmes kept poking his fingers into the wool. After this happened one too many times, Peter politely said, 'If you do that again, next time you might not have any left, Paul!' That really appealed to the crowd.

David stood by Paul and was the consummate diplomat, providing expert commentary, even though he had been denied the glory of shearing Shrek. Peter also handled the situation in true showman style, even if he had needed a little Scotch for fortification.

No world speed records were at stake that night and Peter took his time, carefully avoiding causing Shrek any stress. It took nine minutes to shear Shrek, three times as long as it would normally take to blade shear a sheep, and Shrek took it all in his stride, quietly submitting to Peter's expert hands.

Once Peter had finished his work, lying on the floor was a fleece 4 metres long and more than 1 metre wide. On the scales it weighed 27 kilograms, about six times more than an average merino fleece. If all the fibres that formed his fleece had been joined up end to end, they would have stretched around the world one and a half times.

Despite the harshness of the conditions Shrek had endured for all those years, his fleece was excellent quality. There were no weak spots or breaks, showing he had coped well with the extremes of heat and cold. Tests also showed Shrek's fleece was five years old.

Without his wool it was clear Shrek was in light condition. If Ann hadn't found him, he would have died within months. I was mightily relieved to find he was also a good example of a Bendigo merino, despite being a 19-kilogram featherweight. It would have been very embarrassing to have pictures of a poor specimen beamed to the world's farmers!

As was to be expected, Shrek was a bit wobbly without his giant fleece, so was quickly carried off the stage. Icebreaker agreed to donate $10,000 for the right to make him a triple-layered red merino cover to keep him warm. Emblazoned with Icebreaker's web address, it was a great promotional opportunity and the company had one million hits to its website in 24 hours. Icebreaker went from strength to strength after that.

The shearing beamed live to the world had been a great success, beyond anyone's imagination. It was the top story on the BBC website for three days, second only to an All Blacks game in New Zealand. Wow, eat your heart out, *Coronation Street*!

The archetypal single southern man, Cage had also enjoyed the limelight. In an interview with *Holmes* he said how much he was looking forward to meeting more girls, and he received many offers by phone and email the next day.

That Page-stopping Photo

Stephen Jaquiery

'A man shore a sheep in Cromwell last night, and the whole world watched.'

So penned Dave Cannan, the *Otago Daily Times* chief reporter, the night Shrek was shorn before live audiences on CNN, BBC, Reuters, Channels 7, 9 and 10 (Australia), APTN (Hong Kong) and New Zealand's own TV One. Extraordinary!

All the stars in the cosmos must have aligned before this spectacle, in which a fairly ordinary-looking merino wether, a sheep which avoided being mustered for years, eventually had its fleece removed before an estimated worldwide audience of 1.2 billion people.

One of the quiet pleasures of working for a newspaper is making people famous for a day. Quite often I will photograph an ordinary person in an interesting way and they become the toast of the community for at least as long as it takes for their photo to become fish and chip wrapper.

When I arrived at Bendigo to photograph the sheep with the very large fleece, I saw what looked like a sprung woolpack. The sheep was about the size of a 200-litre drum supported by short legs — I never in my wildest dreams imagined what we were about to kick-start.

To me, the measure of a successful photograph is one that stops casual readers flicking through pages. I knew, with my first few frames of this sheep, that was unlikely to happen. I took photographs of the sprung woolpack by itself and with John. All the while, I was trying very hard to convince John to shear the sheep then and there so I would have a before and after photograph: that would have been page-stopping. But I think even at that early stage, John could see more potential in this sheep than it being just a one-day wonder, and he flatly refused.

When Cage slung the sheep over his

broad shoulders then shook his head out from a bellyful of 30-centimetre-long fleece, there was perhaps more of a wince than a smile on his face. His shoulder was in the sheep's groin, which caused it to empty its bladder on the hapless shepherd right at that moment.

In a personal twist to the story, not too long after Shrek was shorn and money started pouring in for Cure Kids, my second daughter was born. Phoebe, we soon discovered, suffered from a life-threatening condition which needed urgent surgery. Not many years ago, the surgery was unknown, and Phoebe's outlook could have been quite different. It is exactly the kind of medical research paid for by funding from Cure Kids that saved her life. Shrek is loved by many kids. They are his 'mates'. Phoebe is always pleased to see him — she is one of those mates.

Above: Phoebe Jaquiery, with Shrek.

The doors to heritage.

The stone woolshed at Morven Hills — one of New Zealand's largest stone shearing sheds.

In total, the Morven Hills woolshed contained 34 shearing stands, 17 on each side.

I wonder what Shrek's ancestors would think if they saw him today.

Shrek's home at Bendigo was once part of the greater Morven Hills Station, which was home to more than 68,000 sheep.

The Life of Shrek

A trip back to Morven Hills

Chapter 4

Shrek Meets the Prime Minister

Paul Holmes and the world had got what they wanted — to see the renegade caught and shorn. In a little over 10 days Shrek had raised $60,000 for charity. The number-one limited-edition box set of Shrek's wool had sold for a mind-boggling $5000. One of the Shrek tops was auctioned for $10,000.

John Hall, the former chairman of advertising agency Saatchi and Saatchi, estimated that it would have cost more than $100 million to buy the amount of exposure Shrek had generated for Central Otago and New Zealand. As the hottest story in the world for two weeks, Shrek was a marketer's dream, demonstrating the superior thermal properties of merino fibre and combining all the best elements of New Zealand — a lovable rogue surviving in a scenic, pristine and dramatic environment. The media had got in behind the Shrek story, recognising it to be an incredible opportunity to be part of something that had no commercial gain, no hidden message, no controversy.

Not surprisingly, perhaps, the tale of Shrek brought all sorts of rivals out of the woodwork. Four King Country farmers in the North Island claimed to have three Shreks, dubbed 'the Taharoa trio', which they believed were the woolliest sheep in the world. A couple from the backblocks of Victoria, Australia, reckoned that three years earlier they had had a fine merino called Sumo with a 52-centimetre fleece. The *Otago Daily Times* reran a story that had appeared in the *Otago Witness* in 1918 of a hermit wether with a 45-centimetre fleece. Not to be beaten, Rotorua's Agrodome produced a 57-centimetre-long fleece off a Lincoln-cross wether. Then there was the 65-centimetre fleece from a wild merino shot on Ram Island (Motutapu) in Lake Wanaka in 1996. What all the usurpers failed to realise was that it was Shrek's story that had won the hearts of millions, not just the length of his wool. In fact, the rivals simply gave the Shrek story more 'legs', to use a journalistic phrase, and kept the story going for longer.

Now the renegade had been shorn, I was sure nobody would be interested in him. It was back to normal life on the station and if he was lucky Shrek would be put back in a paddock to retire after his brief, albeit intense, experience of stardom.

The morning after the shearing, Shrek was out on the ram shed veranda looking out over the green paddocks, golden vineyards and autumn leaves on the poplar trees — a very different scene to the rocky tops of Bendigo. Although he was still a little shaky, his head was up and he was taking everything in. For the first time he got to have a good look at me — the man he could find blindfolded in a crowd of hundreds within minutes.

For the first time he got to have a good look at me — the man he could find blindfolded in a crowd of hundreds within minutes.

Then, typically, my cellphone rang. Schools in Queenstown wanted Shrek to visit that day. Cage was enjoying the limelight so we agreed to fold down the back seats of the Jeep and take the skinny old wether for a trip to Queenstown, the most glamorous tourist destination in New Zealand. I drove, while Cage sat in the back seat and Shrek in the front, looking out the window.

For a sheep that had been high up in the mountains for so many years, road travel was at times a frightening experience. Going up the winding Kawarau Gorge, a big truck came around the corner towards the Jeep. Shrek ducked sideways, then stood back up, peering out the windscreen again. Then another truck came towards us and Shrek ducked sideways again. Cage said in a dry voice, 'Shrek doesn't know the road rules yet', although by the time we arrived in Queenstown he was more relaxed.

Kids were waiting everywhere to get their photos taken with Shrek. Afterwards we went for a walk downtown. To everybody's amazement, he took the lead like a lab dog out in front of Cage and me. It was totally unexpected. Even though for the two previous weeks he had been surrounded by people, normally a sheep that hadn't been near civilisation for years would be very nervous and flighty, especially on its own without other animals for security. But not Shrek! Without hesitation Shrek popped into radio stations and banks, riding escalators and lifts. Later, when I was having a cup of coffee with Kaye Parker from Cure Kids, I wondered aloud, 'Has there ever been a parliamentary reception held for a sheep? After all, they've been the backbone of our New Zealand economy for so many years.'

Kaye looked at me and said, 'You have gone completely and utterly mad!'

It wasn't the first time I had been told that, but Kaye agreed it would be excellent publicity.

I knew Helen Clark's press secretary so gave him a call and asked him what the PM might think of the idea of a visit from Shrek. David said he would ask her and ring back. An hour later the phone rang. The PM was with the Chilean ambassador in Hamilton that week but how about the following week? Tuesday, 1 pm, on the front steps of Parliament?

'Holy hell,' I said.

Immediately Cure Kids organised their corporate sponsor Qantas to transport Shrek to Wellington at no charge. They agreed to move heaven and earth to make the Wellington visit happen. Meanwhile, Wanaka Joinery made him his own corporate box — lined with red carpet of course!

Cure Kids likes to give children with life-threatening illnesses once-in-a-

Above: Prime Minister Helen Clark, Shrek and I in the midst of a media scrum.

Shrek Meets the PM **79**

lifetime experiences, so 16-year-old Cure Kids ambassador Keeley Jackson from Queenstown was invited to accompany Shrek on his adventure to Wellington. It was a major undertaking for Keeley as she has type-1 diabetes, requires daily insulin injections and constantly needs to check her blood-sugar levels. Despite the difficulties, Keeley was beside herself with excitement at the prospect of meeting Shrek and the Prime Minister. Ann, Cage, Josie Spillane from Cure Kids and I would be going to Wellington too.

The day Shrek flew to Wellington, word spread quickly around the Queenstown airport. We could hardly move for the crowds — it seemed everyone wanted their photo taken with Shrek. The airport staff were fantastic, letting me go out the back to supervise Shrek being loaded into the cargo hold and reassure him everything was okay.

Word spread quickly around the Queenstown airport. We could hardly move for the crowds — it seemed everyone wanted their photo taken with Shrek.

Once we were in the air, the pilot announced there was a very special guest on board. Josie and Keeley were invited to walk up and down the aisle collecting money for Cure Kids.

There was just as much havoc when we arrived at Wellington airport. Again we were so inundated with people we couldn't move. When unloading Shrek, the Maori ground crew started making jokes. 'Hey, Shrek, how about we have a hangi with lamb chops?' No way. Not this sheep!

A Jeep dealership had agreed to supply two new black Jeeps to pick us all up from the airport. Shrek felt very important and so did Cage. Away we went for our 10 am meeting with Helen. As we drove up to Parliament, Cage said, 'Bloody hell, they've put the red carpet out for us, running right down to the long stairs in front of the buildings.' But security staff stopped us as we came up onto the lawn area. 'Sorry. The Chilean ambassador hasn't finished lunch with Helen. You will have to wait.'

The government cars were all lined up in front of the stairs with the paparazzi milling around waiting. Cure Kids had let a couple of schools know Shrek was going to be at Parliament and when they arrived they ran across the lawn shouting his name. Realising Shrek was in the convoy, the paparazzi broke rank, deserting their posts waiting for the ambassador, and quickly formed a media scrum around Shrek's jeep. Flashes were going off as TV celebrities vied to get

Above: Shrek still coming to terms with looking like an ordinary
sheep again, as I indicate the foot-long length of his old fleece
the day after the shearing.

OK SHREK BABY, TODAY YOU'VE GOT NBC AT 7.30AM, BBC AT 8.45AM ...

SHREK

SMITH

▮ HOW THE WORLD SAW SHREK

Shrek has hit the headlines overseas. Here is how some of the international media reported on Shrek the hermit sheep:

● Pulling the wool over his eyes (*Sydney Morning Herald*).

● Super furry sheep finally getting haircut (NBC 10).

● Shrek the sheep faces his shearers (BBC News).

● Monster sheep captured down under (BBC Newsround).

Stardom has its price

By Neal Wallace

Shrek is becoming priceless and may have to be locked away for his own safety.

The hermit merino wether shunned musterers in the Central Otago mountains for the past six years, but the woolly mammoth's exploits have thrust him into the international limelight to such an extent that his owner, John Perriam, says his worthless old wether may be a tempting target for someone.

Since being captured on Bendigo Station last Thursday, Shrek has been kept in small paddocks around the Tarras homestead and in the woolshed. But Mr Perriam said he might have to lock the 9-year-old away.

"I don't want anything to happen to him, when he can do so much good for New Zealand," he said.

In a pure farming sense, Shrek has no monetary value. He is too old to be sold for mutton and his 380mm-long fleece is too long for weaving or spinning machines designed to deal with wool 85mm long.

Normally, he would have been killed for meat when aged about 6 and on today's market would be worth about $40. His wool, with one year's growth, would be worth another $45.

"His fleece is basically worthless in one sense, but from another point, he has one of the most valuable fleeces around," Mr Perriam said.

Mr Perriam was yesterday interviewed by the BBC, the Australian Broadcasting Corporation and other Australian radio stations.

Media in the United States, the United Kingdom and Australia have carried Shrek's tale of survival under headlines such as "Monster sheep captured down under", "Shrek the sheep faces his shearers", "Super furry sheep heading for haircut" and "Pulling the wool over his eyes".

Continued on page 2

the perfect shot of themselves with Shrek. It seemed the people who had been saying, 'What's all the fuss about Shrek? He's just a sheep,' were the ones most determined to get their photos in the history books!

The next thing I knew, I got a tap on the shoulder. 'Hello, John,' a deep husky voice said. 'Oh, hello, Helen,' I replied.

Prime Minister Helen Clark was a very clever lady. With photographers everywhere she quickly saw the opportunity for a feel-good photo and in a flash was posing for the camera down on one knee looking Shrek in the eye. Unfortunately, the Minister of Agriculture also tried to get into the photos by crouching down behind Shrek. He instantly reactivated all the sheep jokes going around Australia about New Zealand sheep-shaggers.

Josie had been trying to impress upon Cage the fact that, as he was representing Cure Kids on this trip, he needed to behave himself. A hungover Cage was nervous about meeting the Prime Minister, so Josie had been coaching him about how to address her.

'What do I say when I meet her?' he'd asked.

'You say, nice to meet you, Prime Minister,' replied Josie.

So everyone had to listen to 'Nice to meet you, Prime Minister' all the way to Wellington!

But when the moment came, he botched it . . . or did he? After meeting her myself, I said, 'I'd like to introduce you to Cage.'

Like some kind of Crocodile Dundee character, the big southern lad took off his cowboy hat, threw away his roll-your-own cigarette, stuck out his hand and said, 'Gidday, Mr President.'

Like some kind of Crocodile Dundee character, the big southern lad took off his cowboy hat, threw away his roll-your-own cigarette, stuck out his hand and said, 'Gidday, Mr President.'

Helen gave Cage her famous Helen stare, said nothing and, with a glint in her eye, turned to talk to the next person. Cage had been 'Helenised' and no one knew what to say. Any bad memories were erased when Neida Simeona from Wellington gave Helen one of the limited-edition boxes of Shrek's wool. At just 10 years of age, Neida had been diagnosed with ovarian cancer. Thanks to Shrek, the now 15 year old was over the moon at being given the chance to give a gift to the Prime Minister.

Meanwhile, the Chilean ambassador waved from his car as his cavalcade quietly exited Parliament Grounds without attracting any media interest at all. It was Shrek's day, the first time in the history of New Zealand that a sheep had upstaged politicians and bureaucrats in the heart of their own territory.

To drive the final nail in the coffin, Maori protesters upset over foreshore and seabed issues were marching in a large hikoi into Wellington that very same day. Helen wouldn't even meet them as they protested outside Parliament and that night, on TV One's *Close Up* programme, the reporter asked the Prime Minister why she was prepared to meet Shrek the sheep and not the Maori hikoi?

'I found Shrek better company,' she replied.

Helen's comment instantly put Shrek back in the headlines and inspired cartoonists. In a pattern that was to be repeated many times, the end of one unique experience had opened up the door to another.

We were due to visit Wellington Hospital that afternoon to meet some seriously ill children. But we had some spare time to fill beforehand, so I suggested we take a quick trip to Kirkcaldie & Stains, New Zealand's premier department store, which was managed by a friend of mine, Richard Holden.

Kirkcaldies is only a short distance from Parliament, so suddenly a sheep with a red coat was walking through the heart of Wellington's golden shopping mile with a party of high country musterers in tow. It was a very strange sight and we soon attracted a huge following of curious shoppers and office workers, creating our own mini hikoi.

Kirkcaldies staff and customers were gobsmacked when Shrek entered the hallowed halls of New Zealand's ultimate shopping destination. It was the first of many left-field surprises Shrek was to throw in the coming years.

Once Shrek had met his fans and browsed the shelves of exclusive brands we headed off to Wellington Hospital. We had organised official permission for the visit but we couldn't find the right entrance and ended up walking up and down the corridors looking for the children's ward. Nothing could have prepared me, Ann and Cage for what we saw. Until this point the whole Shrek phenomenon had been a bit of fun, but when we met those children with life-threatening illnesses it really hit home who we were helping. We saw some really sick children who, through no fault of their own, did not have very bright futures. But, despite their problems, they were still kids and beamed with delight when they met Shrek. His visit had clearly left a bright spot in their dark day.

Ann, Cage and I were pretty sombre afterwards. These children were just a

small representation of the 26,000 kids in New Zealand with life-threatening illnesses. We were very moved and overwhelmed by what we had achieved by finding a sheep on the side of a hill and we were determined to do anything else we could to help these children.

That night we stayed at Richard Holden's upmarket apartment at Oriental Bay overlooking Wellington harbour. Richard had invited lots of friends around to meet his famous house guest. Shrek loved all the attention but when his admirers went upstairs to enjoy a party and left him by himself in his downstairs bedroom with ensuite he was not impressed. Somehow he managed to break out and climb the stairs so he could join in! Everyone was amazed. Shrek was allowed to stay for a while before being put back to bed.

The next day we flew back to Queenstown via Christchurch. On the stopover I let Shrek out of his box to stretch his legs. When Qantas invited us to bring Shrek into the private Qantas Club lounge, you can imagine the surprised looks on the faces of the members when a sheep in a red coat came through the doors.

So far, Shrek had not yet had to answer the call of nature inside but now our luck had just run out. As I was in the middle of a media interview, Shrek did his first little marbles in the middle of the Qantas lounge. In a flash I said to Josie, whom I'd named Jack Russell because of her dogged determination, 'Russell, sort that out, will you?'

It was the first of many such accidents but they always got a laugh. Once, in front of the residents of the Wanaka Retirement Village, Shrek relaxed and had a piddle on the new carpet. 'Don't worry,' said the nurse, 'they all do that around here!'

Above: Shrek meets Jamie Ede at Wellington Hospital. Our hearts went out to all the children at the hospital, many suffering from debilitating illnesses through no fault of their own.

Shrek with Sir Tim Wallis outside Warbirds Over Wanaka.

Silver Fern sharp-shooter Irene van Dyk at the Rotary fundraiser in Timaru.

Former All Black, Graham Thorne, and grandchild pose for a snapshot with Shrek.

Meeting Lotto queen, Hilary Timmins, in Remuera, Auckland.

Shrek very wary of that big, sharp knife at The Grove restaurant in Auckland. The Grove was the Supreme Award winner in the 2010 Metro Audi Restaurant of the Year awards.

Debbie Forrest-Scurr, the Speight's perfect, or nearly perfect, woman 2007, about to start the lolly scramble at Shrek's birthday celebrations. My son Daniel is the pilot.

The Life of Shrek
With other celebrities

Above: Mustering at Bendigo Station. In the background is Mt Pisa and the Upper Clutha Valley.

Chapter 5

On the Road for Charity

The children's ward at Wellington Hospital had been a real eye-opener. Without your health it is very difficult to make your way in life and the visit had made me realise it is too easy to take good health for granted. These seriously ill children had an uphill battle ahead of them and they needed as much help as possible.

I could see that as an official Cure Kids celebrity ambassador, Shrek had the potential to do a lot of good, even though he no longer had his super-long fleece. And if that helped these children, then I was prepared to push the boundaries with the old wether. I didn't know exactly how Shrek could help but I had an open mind and was determined to take every opportunity to capitalise on Shrek's popularity in the name of charity.

Word soon spread that Shrek would attend events if donations were made to Cure Kids. It wasn't long before the phone was ringing. 'Would it be possible for Shrek to visit our retirement home/hospital/school/fundraiser/charity event?' It seemed everyone wanted Shrek at their event. If it was humanly possible I said yes, and fortunately that was the case most of the time.

The requests came from all over New Zealand. Being Shrek's chauffeur and minder would mean spending a lot of time away from Bendigo but fortunately by this time we had a full-time manager to take care of the day-to-day running of the station. Heather was a strong believer in supporting the community and was happy for Shrek to raise money for charity as long as it didn't encroach too much on family life.

One of my passions was showing stud sheep but it soon became obvious that that particular hobby would have to go by the wayside as I wouldn't have time to prepare the animals properly for the show ring or to travel to events. However, seeing the pleasure Shrek gave people quickly became far more rewarding than winning ribbons. Besides, Shrek had taken up residence in the ram shed and he wasn't about to share it, even with his blue-blood cousins.

One of Shrek's first celebrity appearances was an all-expenses-paid trip to the Trentham Races in Wellington. Shrek had only just visited the capital a couple of months earlier to meet the Prime Minister. Race organisers knew he was sure to pull the punters and in return for gracing the event with his presence, Shrek would earn $20,000 for Cure Kids, not to mention having All Black Jonah Lomu's big Ford Mustang at his disposal. Kaye and Josie from Cure Kids were invited and for once Heather came along too.

Since we were going to the races, Shrek had to be dressed appropriately, so there was great excitement at Queenstown airport when he arrived wearing a new winner's red cover with gold lining, specially embroidered with the Trentham logo. Before he was loaded on the plane, Qantas let our party out on the tarmac for a group photo to mark the occasion. To everyone's amazement,

Above: As an official Cure Kids ambassador, Shrek meets children from all over the country. I never get tired of seeing the delight on people's faces when they meet him. It makes being his travel companion incredibly rewarding.

for some reason Kaye decided it was a good idea to take Shrek's lead off. Oh no! Shrek was loose on the tarmac, but as he was to show us time after time, he likes being with people. There was no sudden dash for freedom. In fact, Shrek didn't move an inch while we hurriedly put his lead back on. From then on Kaye was no longer deemed to be a suitable lead holder!

At Trentham Shrek had a special marquee with hay and a white picket fence, but he spent most of the day being led and mobbed by children of all ages and making guest appearances in the bird cage. I'm not sure if Shrek is a great racing fan. Although he loved the kids, most of the punters seemed a little intoxicated later in the day and he wasn't very impressed having champagne spilt over him. But it was just another day at the office for Shrek.

Near the end of the day we were invited to the president's lounge to watch the last race, 'Shrek Flies Qantas'. Shrek was left loose in his fenced marquee. Josie was concerned he might get out but I told her not to worry. 'It's fine, he'll stay put and eat his hay.'

A few months later at the Auckland Pet Expo, Shrek did break out of his pen in the middle of the night and created havoc, leading an uprising of goats and pigs. There was a huge tangle in the morning, but it was worth the hassle because Shrek earned another $20,000 for Cure Kids and was in the esteemed company of other celebrities, including New Zealand's own Lionman Craig Busch and All Black Carlos Spencer's cat. Needless to say, Shrek was a very tired boy at the end of that trip after being poked and pulled for endless photos and then staying up all night!

Back in Queenstown, Shrek was invited to make a guest appearance at the Coronet Peak international 16-hour ski race. The mountains are Shrek's home and he had a great time in the snow with Cure Kids ambassadors, sponsors, race competitors and the public, and of course everyone laughed when he left a patch of golden snow as a souvenir of his visit! That night at the welcome dinner it felt good to present Cure Kids with a $60,000 cheque for the money Shrek had raised so far. I also endeared myself further to Josie by calling her Jack Russell in front of all the corporate sponsors she was trying to impress. In time she was to get her own back, calling me Grandpapa of Shrek — a name that gave Heather huge pleasure!

Shrek was invited to all sorts of crazy events. The Accor $10 Challenge involved 35 teams of two competitors finding ways to travel from Auckland to

SHREK

Above: Arthur Chapman-Cohen with Shrek in a purpose-built cave at the Wanaka A&P Show.

Queenstown in three days on just $10. They paid $7000 per team for the privilege and completed various challenges along the way. The final one was to arrive in Queenstown in a unique way. Two competitors decided to dress up like Elvis and arrive with Shrek in the back of their Jeep. They didn't win the race but caused a huge stir when they arrived outside the five-star Sofitel Queenstown Hotel accompanied by a busking bagpiper roped in from outside a nearby store, just to add some ambience. The newly appointed Australian general manager didn't know what to make of these mad Kiwis! I had to tell everyone to stand back as it was chaos. Once again Shrek had stolen the show and the manager said, 'It could only happen in New Zealand.'

Not all the events were about raising money. In 2005 Cure Kids ran its first 'Ticket to Hope', which involved treating 15 very ill children and a parent for an all-expenses-paid weekend to Queenstown. For a few precious days these children could experience the thrill of living in the moment and not being different. It also gave their parents the chance to share their experiences with other people in the same situation, in an environment far away from hospital corridors. Many of the kids had never seen a sheep before so when Shrek visited them at the Novotel it was a huge thrill to meet the most famous sheep in New Zealand — even more exciting than meeting the TV and radio personality Lana Coc-Kroft.

Later that year Shrek was invited to a Rotary charity dinner and auction in Timaru along with Silver Ferns New Zealand netball great Irene van Dyk. Timaru is only a few hours' drive from Bendigo so I put Shrek in the back of the Jeep and off we went over the Lindis. I hate turning up early at an event so decided to stop for a coffee to fill in time. I left the keys in the ignition and the vehicle unlocked but didn't think it would be a problem because who was likely to steal a vehicle with the most famous sheep in New Zealand inside? However, as fate would have it, there was a problem because somehow Shrek managed to lock the doors and set the security alarms going. Of course I couldn't open the vehicle because the keys were still in the ignition. It was very embarrassing explaining to the Automobile Association's roadside assistance service that I was locked outside my Jeep by a sheep. Meanwhile, Shrek just peered out the window as if to say, 'Let's get going!' Shrek sure would have been sent to the dog tucker paddock if he hadn't had to make an appearance that night!

I always like to push the boundaries, so decided it would be a good idea to

Above: Shrek, looking the part with Cure Kids on the slopes of the Coronet Peak Ski Field, Queenstown.

take Shrek's special life-sized polystyrene cave to the dinner. It had been made for the Auckland Pet Expo and was the ideal backdrop for Shrek photos. The cave wasn't the easiest thing to transport or set up and Josie reckoned it looked a bit like Santa's grotto but it was hugely popular with the guests. Irene van Dyk has very long legs and was wearing a very short netball skirt when Shrek took her into his cave while I tried to look elsewhere.

The after-dinner speeches were projected onto a big screen, but when I spoke the cameras were naturally focused on Shrek. I like to tell a good yarn but when my stories got a bit long-winded, unbeknown to me Shrek lay down and went to sleep. The crowd went into hysterics and I was so embarrassed because, of course, I didn't get the joke. I guess Shrek had heard my stories all before. For the second time in one day Shrek was destined for the dog tucker paddock but was saved by the diary full of upcoming events. Cure Kids was happy anyway because the auction raised another $50,000.

Another time Shrek got the last laugh was at Waikaia's Whitestone Cheese Rolling event. For sheer fun, few events can rival chasing a cheese down a hill, and everybody of any age group can take part. Shrek was in a great mood that day and was out the door of his house, down the steps and jumping in the back of the Jeep, as quick as a flash. He hadn't been out in public for a week and I could see he was full of anticipation about yet another adventure.

I drove down through Roxborough into northern Southland, getting horribly lost on the back roads to Waikaia, while Shrek enjoyed looking at the horses, cattle and sheep we passed by. We arrived to find the crowd shouting and cheering as country and western singer Suzanne Prentice started the desperate housewives race. Then the jewellery magnate Michael Hill began another race. Next it was Shrek's turn. His race was for eight- and nine-year-old kids and there were about 50 entrants. There was a false start when some eager kids broke the barrier and had to be brought back behind the starting line.

The music was up loud and Shrek was starting to get really wound up, pulling on the end of the lead rope I was holding. We let the cheese go and off the kids all went down the first steep section of the 300-metre hill, with no hope of catching the cheese. Shrek just about pulled the lead out of my hand. I could see he was in the mood

Startled kids were awestruck as this sheep in a red cover, with 0800 Cure Kids written on the side, galloped past them.

to race and rather than me having a heart attack trying to keep up with the kids, I unclicked the lead and away he went.

At 50 metres he was passing kids and jumping over the ones who had fallen over on the slope. By 200 metres he had the front runners in his sights, some of whom were starting to catch up to the cheese ball as it slowed on the gentler lower slope. The long row of spectators strung out down the hill was shouting encouragement. Startled kids were awestruck as this sheep in a red cover, with 0800 Cure Kids written on the side, galloped past them.

Shrek got to the lead just before the first kid made a lunge for the grand prize and so he rewrote the books as the first celebrity to start and win a race. Mind you, Michael Hill or Suzanne Prentice could be forgiven, even though they were half his age in equivalent human years. Shrek had four legs and they only had two!

Standing at the top of the hill looking down, Shrek and the mob of kids away in the distance below us reminded me of a pack of hounds that had just caught their prey. And as the cheese ball was carried back to the judge amongst a large crowd, Shrek claimed his prize with the kids.

Shrek was a tired boy that afternoon and slept most of the way back to Bendigo. It was almost as if he knew what he was doing and got a lot of satisfaction out of these fundraising excursions. I certainly did!

Rural people really relate to Shrek and his story because they understand the need to make the most of what Mother Nature deals up. I guess that is part of life in the country. So every few months he would be asked to open an A&P Show

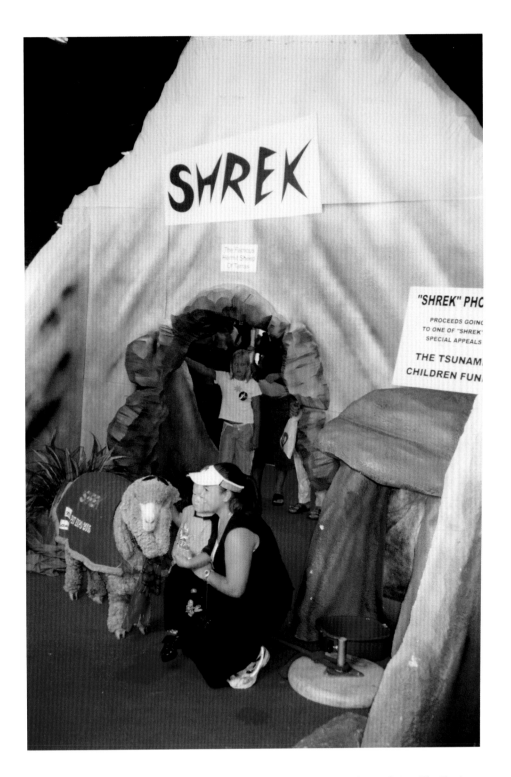

Above: Shrek posing patiently for photos at the Auckland Pet Expo in front of his special life-sized polystyrene cave. The cave wasn't the easiest thing to move about but it was hugely popular.

and judge all sorts of entries. Of course I was always asked to go along as well, but knew that he was the guest and I was simply the chauffeur!

At Oamaru he led the award parade with the granddaughter of the president while I ate scones with the life members. At Taieri, outside Dunedin, he arrived by Westpac rescue helicopter and landed in the middle of the ring with a large crowd waiting. Even Prime Minister Helen Clark wouldn't get such a royal welcome! Shrek just took it all in his stride. The local Wanaka show was of course a big one for Shrek. He attended two years in a row but the one thing he didn't like was the Jack Russell race. Those little dogs are not to be trusted.

The Chertsey Woolly Munchers festival in mid Canterbury was a complete washout. The organisers had invited celebrities to come along, including the flamboyant chef Peta Mathias, humourist Jim Hopkins and, of course, that superstar sheep called Shrek! Anticipating a hot summer's day, the organisers had provided a few tents for shade, but they were very inadequate for sheltering against the howling southerly wind and rain that arrived instead.

Peta drew the best straw, being provided with a large marquee for her cooking demonstrations. Locals and holidaymakers alike crowded around in their raincoats as she cooked up delicious-smelling lamb dishes. Shrek had been allocated a small gazebo in a far corner of the field. Trudging across the sodden

Above: Lucy Perriam and the Chapman-Cohen twins on stage at Shrek's twelfth birthday party.

grass was a rather uninviting prospect, so the obvious solution was to join Peta in the marquee. Shrek was unimpressed and soon lay down like a dog among the crowd and went to sleep.

Once everyone had given him a pat and taken a photo I decided it was time for us to head away up to Christchurch to visit my good friend Grant Calder. A merino farmer from Lauder in Central Otago, Grant was a patient at the spinal unit at Burwood Hospital after his farm quad bike had rolled on top of him.

Grant is an outstanding dog man, having won three New Zealand and five South Island huntaway and heading dog trial championship titles. His biggest thrill of all was wearing a black blazer with a silver fern, representing New Zealand at dog trials in Australia. So when Grant lost the use of both legs and one arm in the accident, he also lost what he calls 'the right to run'. A visit from Shrek was bound to lift Grant's spirits.

It was still torrential rain when we pulled up in the Jeep. From previous experience I knew trying to get Shrek into the hospital wouldn't be easy if I took

Above: Shrek celebrating his birthday in style.   On the Road for Charity **101**

the official route because some bureaucrats see animals as a health risk despite the huge positive mental health benefits they bring to patients. It would take weeks of bureaucracy to get the right paperwork, so I decided to use the element of surprise instead.

Unannounced, we walked through the front doors of the ward, Shrek leading the way on his red rope and wearing his red coat. He marched straight down the wide shiny vinyl corridor past reception. A staff member leapt to his feet, 'What the bloody hell is this?' he said.

'Shrek is going to see Grant Calder,' I said as I kept on walking. There are wide blue stripes on the vinyl and by now to amuse himself Shrek was jumping each one. As we disappeared down the corridor the receptionist thankfully decided to turn a blind eye to the lack of paperwork for this unauthorised four-legged visitor.

Word spread quickly and soon patients were being wheeled out of their rooms to see the celebrity sheep. Like royalty, Shrek would stop at each wheelchair to greet the patient, whom he'd give a quick nuzzle then move on. It still makes me a little emotional to recall the pleasure the old wether gave those people that had been dealt one of life's cruellest blows. There is a saying on the wall, 'Don't let the things you can't do stop you doing the things you can do,' but of course that is much easier said than done.

Grant and his wife Robyn were staying in a self-care unit on the hospital grounds so, as soon as we could, Shrek and I made a dash through the rain to their place. Looking out the window at the pouring rain, Grant couldn't believe what he was seeing. Once inside, Shrek lay down at Robyn's feet like a faithful dog and fell asleep while we spent an hour or so together. Grant tells me the visit was hugely special. His whole life had revolved around merinos and after being away from the station for so long it was magic just to be able to smell and touch a merino again. He knew he would never again muster the hills but spending time with Shrek helped him deal with this loss.

Grant tells me that after we left he popped into the ward to visit other patients, who kept coming up to him and asking, 'Was that really Shrek?' As always, there were sceptics who doubted the Shrek story, saying it must be 'ballyhoo' but Grant knew Shrek's story was true and defended his reputation.

That day was one of the most memorable of my incredible journey with Shrek. I can't find the words to describe what happened when Shrek visited Grant, but

guest of honour and enjoyed all the attention, walking up and down the main aisle looking at what was on everyone's plate. The guests couldn't believe it!

Josie had a real soft spot for Bendigo, and her boyfriend Mitch loves hunting in the high country, so when the couple decided to get married, guess where they wanted to hold the reception? Josie felt it was a very big favour to ask so for once she was tongue-tied when she and Kaye came to visit one day. Kaye led the conversation: 'There is a very nervous Josie here who wants to ask you a question.'

Somehow Josie managed to blurt out, 'Could Mitch and I get married at Bendigo?'

Kaye had already whispered in my ear and Heather and I were delighted to host the reception. But I didn't want to make it too easy for her!

'Why would you want to get married at Bendigo, Jack?'

The poor girl tried to stutter out her answers, so Heather and I quickly put her out of her misery.

Above: Shrek asleep with Grant and Robyn Calder. Life can be cruel sometimes, but Grant has built a new life, and in doing so, has become an inspiration to all around him.

'Yes, of course, we would love you to get married at Bendigo. The place is yours! Do whatever you like!'

Josie was thrilled but in the next breath said, 'Shrek is not coming to the wedding. I'm not going to be upstaged by a sheep on my big day!'

'We'll see,' I thought, but said nothing.

The service was held at the beautiful old Tarras church where Heather played the organ every Sunday for decades. Then it was back to Bendigo for cocktails in the newly restored original homestead and the reception dinner in the woolshed. Josie had woven her magic again, transforming the place with fabric and fairy lights. She was enjoying all the attention when guess who walked in? Suddenly nobody was looking at the bride any more. You should have seen the look on Josie's face.

'Get that sheep out of here,' she ordered goodnaturedly.

Shrek's response was to answer the call of nature! Of course I was secretly pleased Shrek had yet again upstaged the main event. All the guests wanted a photo taken with Shrek. Then, figuring if you can't beat 'em, join 'em, Josie and Mitch had wedding photos taken with Shrek too.

In my after-dinner speech, I talked about how our friendship had evolved

Above: Celebrating 150 years of Totara Estate, the site of the first frozen meat shipments out of New Zealand. This historic farm is a stark reminder to Shrek how his ancestors became (and remain) vitally significant to the New Zealand economy.

over the years and confessed I now considered Josie a second daughter. Heather thought it was wonderful, although I later found out that Josie and Heather had had a good laugh at my expense that Grandpapa was softening in his older age. I have nothing but respect for Josie's drive and determination to push the boundaries and make a difference in the world.

Above: Josie Spillane, Cure Kids regional manager for the South Island and Fiji, on her wedding day. It was a wonderful day, as Josie and I have become good friends over the years. Shrek, however, looks totally unimpressed at not being the star of the show.

Shrek Travels in Style

Shrek may have lived in a cave for years, but once he joined the human race he expected to travel in style. Most sheep are moved around New Zealand in a stock truck or, at best, in a trailer. But that would be unheard of for Shrek!

The day Shrek was found on the top of Bendigo he was squeezed into the back of the Hilux. Ever since then he has had the priority use of my blue Jeep Cherokee and for long trips he flies Qantas in his specially designed crate lined with red carpet.

Like any pet dog travelling in a car, at first he felt the best place to be was looking out the front window with his feet on the automatic gear shift. For obvious safety reasons we had to convince him the rear compartment was a better place.

Even when he finally relented and agreed to travel in the back it caused issues because following traffic would tailgate us trying to take photos. They'd even follow us into gas stations and try to stop us on the highway.

The day we flew from Queenstown to Wellington to meet the Prime Minister, we made an appearance at a Presbyterian gala at Wanaka first. We

Above: Harriet Rivers and Flynn.

were running late for the flight so 120 kilometres per hour seemed quite slow as we headed over the windy Crown Range to Queenstown. Then we heard the dreaded sound of a siren and saw the unwelcome sight of flashing lights in the rear-vision mirror. Shrek was not concerned when the officer pulled us over and proceeded to ask why we were exceeding the speed limit. I thought, 'Will I or won't I?'

'Actually, officer,' I said. 'Shrek is on his way to meet the Prime Minister for a parliamentary reception and I think they are holding the flight for us in Queenstown.'

The officer looked at me as if I was insane and I thought it's going to be handcuffs time then, mate. He walked around to back of the Jeep and I quickly saw my chance, flicked open the rear glass window and Shrek did the rest, turning on the charm.

Within a minute we were on our way with police escort and no speeding ticket. I looked at Shrek with his expressionless, aloof manner and said, 'Bloody hell, mate, that was close.'

Over the years Shrek would instinctively know that whenever the blue Jeep backed up to the steps of his complex, he was off on another exciting adventure. He would literally run out and jump in the back of the Jeep.

Heather had a very benevolent attitude about Shrek, especially when it came to sharing the same vehicle. On one occasion we both took Shrek on a five-hour trip to Christchurch. I could have sworn he had been at a duck shooters' dinner the night before because he farted all the way as if he had eaten and drunk too much. That was it for Heather. She had to put up with Shrek on the return trip to Bendigo but after that they never shared the same vehicle ever again — the blue Jeep became Shrek's own, with his own personalised MERINO number plate.

On long trips he eventually lies down and goes to sleep but most of the time he watches the countryside and his cousins grazing in the paddocks along the highway. But when arriving at a venue, like an old rock star, he instinctively composes himself, puts his head up and jumps out of the Jeep ready to meet and greet. Even when he flew into the Taieri showgrounds by helicopter, he came out from under the rotors like a fired-up bull.

Thanks to Qantas, Shrek has more frequent flyer points than most New Zealanders.

After landing at Wanaka in a private jet, Shrek waits patiently with Daniel and Christina for his helicopter ride back to Bendigo. Do all celebrities get treated this well?

Ann Scanlan gets to join in on the fun.

An iconic sheep with a Westpac Rescue Helicopter, an iconic lifesaver in New Zealand. Paramedic Bruce Kerr is on the left and pilot Steve Oliver to the right.

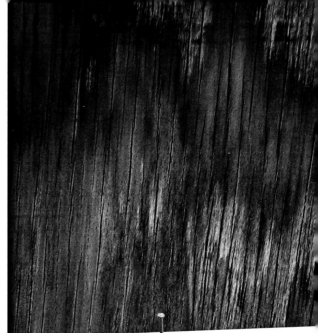

The big Hummerzine that met us at Auckland airport before the Sky Tower shearing

Shrek testing out the Auckland bus service.

The Life of Shrek
Moving in style

Above: An old hotel lays silent after surviving years of rowdy and unruly goldminers in the late 1800s. Welshtown, Bendigo.

Chapter 6

Shrek's Friends at Tarras School

When Shrek was captured, it seemed everyone in the district wanted to see him and that included the 13 pupils down the road at Tarras Primary School, so it wasn't long before they jumped on the school bus and made the visit to Bendigo. Like all children, they were taken by Shrek's gentle nature and his story, so when they got back to the classroom they were soon busy writing.

Like many small country schools, the little school at Tarras struggled financially because funding is partially linked to the roll size. Constantly facing the threat of closure, the volunteer Friends of Tarras School group was always looking for ways to raise funds to keep the school afloat and pay for any extras required to give the children a good education like their city peers.

So it was no surprise when the group floated the idea of publishing a book about Shrek as a fundraiser. It would make a great Christmas present if they could get it ready in time. They didn't know much about publishing but I thought this was a great idea. The rural financial services company FMG agreed to underwrite the costs of publishing the book and Meat & Wool New Zealand donated cash.

The book would be written by the children through their own eyes, starting with Shrek's

Constantly facing the threat of closure, the volunteer Friends of Tarras School group was always looking for ways to raise funds to keep the school afloat.

early life at Bendigo station, his journey to the mountains above, finding his cave and making it home, and then his discovery and road to fame.

As luck would have it a very talented local artist, Jenny Chisholm, put her hand up to do the illustrations. Working under considerable time pressure, she shut herself in a caravan for a month while her husband did the household chores and looked after their two small children. The students of the school even took their turn with baby-sitting duties. The result was amazing — Jenny's drawings superbly capture the character of Shrek and the beauty of the local landscape.

The Friends of Tarras School did all the preliminary computer work, giving Taieri Print in Dunedin the material for the last stages of production. It was an enormous project and when the daughter of one volunteer said to her mother, 'What was life like before Shrek?', her mother replied that she wasn't really sure as the wonderful train of events started by Shrek seemed to dominate life.

The only hurdle now was getting permission from Dreamworks to publish a book about Shrek. There was great relief and excitement the day Nicki Crabbe, the school bus driver, came racing in announcing Dreamworks had given the project the green light. Not much work was done at school the rest of that day!

No one had any idea how successful the book would be so the initial print run was 8000 copies, including 2000 translated into Japanese, such had been the interest in Japan over the Shrek story.

Shrek and the children travelled to Taieri Print to see the book come off the press. Shrek's bag was packed with his favourite oat mix when the school bus and kids turned up at around 9 am to pick him up for the big adventure. He needed a big push-up by Nicki, then Shrek was up in the back of the bus with his mates Arthur and Rupert and all the other schoolchildren.

As the children watched the books come off the printing machines, Shrek spent the afternoon signing copies with his hoof. That night, for a special treat, the kids had takeaways for dinner while Shrek ate his special oat mix. He eventually fell asleep in the motel room while Rupert and Arthur watched TV. It had been the first of many successful outings for Shrek in his involvement with Tarras School.

The day before the book's official launch at Tarras, the entire school and Shrek travelled to Cromwell, as Shrek's friend Helen Clark was in town and the kids wanted to present her with a copy of the book and calendar.

On launch day a chauffer-driven stretch limo pulled up at Shrek's Bendigo house at 1.30 pm. His personalised MERINO number plates were fitted and away Shrek went to Tarras to launch his own book, looking a 'mass of dash'.

A huge crowd of over 250 people was waiting and the limo had trouble getting through to the school. People from all over Otago had turned up. You would have thought Michael Jackson had arrived, not just an old wether from Bendigo.

It was a great community atmosphere with the mayor dressed up with gold chains around his neck, speeches, kids' games and, of course, the book which

was destined to be a runaway success. That Christmas *Shrek the Famous Hermit Sheep of Tarras* was the top-selling children's book at PaperPlus stores nationwide, selling over 50 per cent more copies than any other children's book. Six months later the school was up to its third print run as the Dymocks book chain also wanted to stock the book.

As publishers of the only Shrek book, for several years the school was inundated with requests from people wanting to know what had happened to Shrek. Was he still alive? Yes, he most certainly was, so the school decided to publish a sequel. *Further Adventures of Shrek: New Zealand's Celebrity Sheep* was published in December 2007. This time the children helped their principal Noelene Pullar relate the story by writing letters to Shrek, asking him to tell stories about his adventures since his discovery at the top of Bendigo. Artist and former Tarras School teacher Lesley Faulks illustrated and designed the book and the children created artworks for the inside cover. The second book was launched on Shrek's 12th birthday at Bendigo in the woolshed in front of TV cameras.

Of the two books the original *Shrek the Famous Hermit Sheep of Tarras* has been the most successful, with over 40,000 copies sold in New Zealand to visitors from all parts of the world. After nearly six years it still holds the prime

Above: Tarras School children read Shrek his first book, straight from the presses at Taieri Print. *Shrek: The famous hermit sheep of Tarras* had sold over 40,000 copies by 2010.

spot at the Queenstown airport and is also in hot demand at The Merino Shop, next door to the Tarras School, along with many PaperPlus stores throughout the country. Friends of Tarras School continues to market the book, taking orders and packaging them from the very cramped quarters of the Tarras School staffroom. When they can, local residents help transport boxes of books to reduce courier costs.

To date the Shrek books have raised more than $100,000 for Tarras School, probably making it one of the wealthiest small schools per capita in New Zealand. The school has been able to afford an extra teacher, more sports lessons and equipment, more school trips and more new technology. There is now more than one computer per two students and the aim is for pupils to have a computer each.

Principal Noeline Pullar says publishing and marketing the Shrek books has opened many doors for the students, providing them with opportunities to meet and present themselves to a variety of organisations and groups of people. Visitors from many parts of the country want to meet them, and the children

Above: The front cover of *Shrek: The famous hermit sheep of Tarras*, illustrated by Jenny Chisholm.

have often been asked to sign their names on the books. They certainly feel like celebrities themselves.

It has all been great fun. One day Shrek was asked to come up to the school and help the kids entertain a group from the retirement home at Alexandra. First of all, Shrek lined up with the kids in the classroom while the book was read aloud. Then a haka was performed by the students, which was more up Shrek's alley. With all his mates on each side of him the kids started stamping their feet, each time getting a little closer to the elderly in wheelchairs as they laid down the haka challenge. Then, to everybody's absolute amazement, Shrek started stamping his feet too and advancing along with Arthur and Rupert towards a petrified elderly lady. All was forgiven, as by this stage the teachers were in hysterics laughing at Shrek's antics. As usual he signed several books.

I think the Shrek story is great for kids because it is about never giving up hope, even if you get lost. Shrek and the success of his books are also good examples of how it doesn't matter how small you are — if you take the opportunities around you, anything is possible. In fact, Shrek is living proof that nothing is impossible.

Above: The big book launch. Shrek arrived in a stretch limousine and met the mayor of Central Otago, Malcolm McPherson. If only all book launches were as fancy!

Jenny Chisholm © artist

More of Jenny's great illustrations from Shrek: The famous hermit sheep of Tarras.

Shrek and his friends at Tarras School.

The Life of Shrek

First book

124 Shrek: The story of a Kiwi icon   **Above**: Like fleas on the back of an elephant, our figures are tiny atop this massive piece of Mother Nature which was already breaking up as it floated along in international waters.

Chapter 7

Shearing on an Iceberg

e had some great years travelling around the country raising funds and the profile of Cure Kids. New Zealand's biggest corporates were at Shrek's beck and call and at times he was earning more for an appearance than an All Black or many other celebrities — $20,000 was his standard fee.

Shrek's welfare was always the top priority and he wanted for nothing. If Shrek was not well or seemed to be distressed in any way then plans just had to change. Sadly, many New Zealanders now have little connection with farming. So it was not really surprising when, in 2006, two years after the first shearing, animal welfare activists started making noises about Shrek needing to be shorn again. Shrek was living a life of luxury and was not at all concerned at having a two-year-old fleece. But the letters to the editor said it was setting a bad example to people with sheep on lifestyle blocks.

Of course the first shearing had been an international event thanks to *Holmes* and other media. I knew we couldn't top that so I talked to Cure Kids about holding a special day at Bendigo for Shrek's second shearing. When they rang back and said they were very sorry but didn't have the time and resources to help, I must say I felt a bit dejected.

After the phone call I decided to go for a drive up my old haunt, Loop Road. For once I had the radio turned on and happened to hear on the news that icebergs from Antarctica were floating off the Dunedin coast.

'What the hell,' I thought. 'That'd be a novelty.'

When I rang Stephen Jaquiery at the *Otago Daily Times*, the conversation went something like this.

'Stephen, John Perriam here. I have an idea.'

'You want to shear Shrek on an iceberg,' he immediately and correctly replied. However, he discounted the idea just as quickly.

'Impossible. They are far too dangerous.'

'Oh, well, it was just an idea! Maybe we'll have to shear him in the shed after all.'

Stephen was speaking from experience. He had landed on the iceberg the previous day. Stepping onto the smooth, glassy surface, he had experienced an overwhelming feeling of suspense, as if the whole thing could break up at any moment. When the helicopter backed away, the air was filled with loud reports, like rifle shots, as the berg moved and cracked. The sea slopped and washed its base smooth and a trail of growlers marked its path. This iceberg may have taken thousands of years to form, but as it drifted into warmer waters it was quite obvious that it was not much longer for this world.

The icebergs were generating enormous interest. Helicopters and aircraft flew punters out to sea from dawn to dusk, as often as they could reload. Commercial passenger aircraft diverted from normal routes to give their passengers (or, more likely, their pilots) a look, and civil aviation officials drew up iceberg flight rules.

It was only after a week of more flights out to other icebergs as they drifted past the coast of Otago — and some careful consideration — that Stephen phoned me back and said, 'Maybe, just maybe, as long as the right iceberg arrives.'

As one set of icebergs drifted north and melted, another set drifted up from the

Above: When we saw the three massive bergs coming into sight, they looked like ghosts on the horizon. At that point I had a feeling this wasn't one of my best ideas.

south to take its place. It was during an exploratory flight with Graeme Gale from Helicopters Otago one evening that Stephen saw a very large, very flat iceberg. It looked a suitable iceberg upon which to shear a sheep.

But the weather forecast indicated stormy weather was approaching, and the drifting iceberg would soon be out of reach of the helicopter. There was a window of two days at most. That's when I got a call from a very excited Stephen. 'We'll meet you at the Taieri airport at 10 tomorrow morning,' he said. 'Do you want one helicopter or two?'

Although I knew the cost would be high, I reluctantly agreed to two. It was just too dangerous to rely on one helicopter because the berg was over 100 kilometres out in international waters. Stephen thought someone from the production company Natural History New Zealand might like to join us on the flight. As it turned out they were making a programme on global warming and needed some extra footage. They agreed to share the cost of the choppers as long as high-definition cameras were fitted to the skids.

This was a good start but I needed more help, so I rang Shrek's good friend Jeremy Moon of Icebreaker, who had paid $10,000 to put the red cover on Shrek when he was first shorn. He would put up the rest of the necessary funding. The money situation was sorted.

I rang Cure Kids to let them know what was happening. They understood the stunt was a calculated risk and we wouldn't do anything that would seriously endanger anyone, but they were still relieved not to be invited!

Of course I also needed to get a shearer who was prepared to shear a sheep on an iceberg. I knew just the man! Jimmy Barnett had blade-shorn Bendigo stud sheep for years and would be perfect for the job. He can be a hard character to track down but, as luck would have it, he was in cellphone range when I called.

'What are you doing tomorrow, Jimmy?'

'Just digging the wife's garden in Oamaru to earn some brownie points.'

'What about shearing Shrek for us on an iceberg?'

'That sounds interesting,' he said. He truly was a laid-back character — and just as well, we were soon to discover.

The iceberg was bound to capture the imagination of adults but we also wanted to come up with an idea that would appeal to kids. That's when our landgirl Harriet Rivers came up with the idea of making Shrek a set of crampons for the ice. The local engineer Matt Robinson got no sleep that night, but the crampons are a work of art and are on display at the House of Shrek in Tarras.

The night before the iceberg trip Heather and I went to Arrowtown to share a meal with friends and some visiting American scientists. The conversation turned to Shrek and the following day's adventure. The Americans agreed it would be very exciting but warned that icebergs are huge crystals. Under no circumstances should we drive anything into the ice because even a small scratch can start a major fracture.

The flight out to the iceberg took about an hour. Shrek sat in the back with me while I looked out the window and spotted killer whales. The pilots were more interested in a storm that was headed up from the south. If it hit after we were

Above: Shrek waits, unfazed, like a big seal.

dropped off on the iceberg they wouldn't be able to pick us up again and we'd probably be swept into the sea. Not the most inspiring news!

Then, on the horizon, we saw three massive ghostlike objects. As we got closer the size and colour of the water around them was stunning. They looked so majestic from the air.

The aircraft carrier berg had a high pointed nose and a flat area the size of a football field. We could only see about 20 per cent of it because the rest was underwater. There was a very nervous tone in my voice when we descended and the pilots told us to get out while the helicopter was still at full power in case the berg started to break up.

As the chopper flew away we were left alone, like fleas on the back of an elephant. Jimmy, Stephen, a TV cameraman, me, and of course Shrek were floating on this massive piece of Mother Nature. Even with crampons on, the ice was so slippery that Shrek immediately sat down like a big slug.

Just then a loud noise

To my horror I realised it was the iceberg splitting way down in the sea below us.

like lightning rang out. I immediately thought the storm had struck but to my horror I realised it was the iceberg splitting way down in the sea below us. With a massive convulsion, a huge piece of the berg broke off.

By now the helicopters were well up in the sky and Stephen was shouting on the two-way radio to get us off the iceberg because it was breaking up. I looked at Jimmy and said, 'I don't think this was one of my better ideas.' But then the berg seemed to settle down and Jimmy said in a slow drawl, 'We may as well get on and shear Shrek.'

We had brought a large woollen Fernmark rug with us to shear Shrek on, so we quickly unrolled it and Jimmy got cracking. It was the longest half hour of my life. All sorts of things were racing around my head. Mainly that I was responsible if we all got crushed in the ocean by millions of tonnes of jagged ice. I could just imagine the headline: 'Shrek Lost at Sea as Massive Berg Breaks Up. Four People Also Perished But Will Be Named at a Later Date.'

I drew some comfort from the helicopters flying around overhead, but I knew if our berg rolled over or even lurched on an angle, which they do all the time, we wouldn't survive falling 30 metres over the edge into the sea.

Finally, Jimmy finished shearing Shrek and it was time to pack up. I had turned my back on Stephen and was horrified to hear the 'thonk, thonk, thonk'

of something being hammered into the ice. It was an *Otago Daily Times* flagpole. In all the excitement and drama I'd forgotten to tell Stephen that was exactly the sort of thing we shouldn't do!

The tourist flights to the 'Shrekberg' started early the next morning. Pilots radioed back a message that a massive piece of ice was missing from the exact spot where Stephen had driven in the pole. The American scientists were right, but luckily the berg hadn't broken up while we were still on it.

Having solid ground under my feet and a Speight's in my hand back at the Taieri pub later that day was a huge relief. When a bloke came into the pub and asked Jimmy, 'Where have you been today?', he replied 'Aw, just over the coast a bit.'

The *Otago Daily Times* photos of Shrek being shorn on the ice made headlines around the world. In hindsight the stunt was a crazy thing to do but the berg shearing had paid off and my phone rang hotter than ever with requests for Shrek to make appearances at charity fundraisers.

Above: I forgot to tell Stephen not to hammer anything into the ice as it could cause the berg to crack. Within 12 hours, the steel standard and the ODT flag were at the bottom of the ocean.

Shrek on Ice

Stephen Jaquiery

After the initial shearing in front of the world, the *Otago Daily Times* continued with some coverage of Shrek — usually on the inside pages — but its news directors largely saw him as a woolly anomaly which had outlasted reader interest.

What they did not see, however, is how Shrek continued to captivate an audience: how he could walk into a gathering of elderly people and sit down — amazing them just by being relaxed and un-sheeplike; or how he would go to a summer show and be the major drawcard, for both young and old.

It would take something special for Shrek to make the front page of the *Otago Daily Times* again. Well, he did, and it was special, but boy did it take some good luck. The stars really needed to align for Shrek to be successfully shorn on ice.

After the event Dave Cannan put pen to paper in the *Otago Daily Times*: 'A man shore a sheep on an iceberg yesterday — and no, I'm not making this up.'

The only reason for shearing Shrek on an iceberg had been to generate national, and hopefully also international, publicity for his charity Cure Kids. I could look after the newspaper commitments, but we did not have room to take film crews from both New Zealand TV broadcasters out to the iceberg. Instead, we agreed to hire an independent cameraman who made his shearing footage available to both TV One and TV3 for that night's news. I purposely left it until quite late the day before the shearing to notify the TV crews. It was a fair bet they would be interested in covering the

story, but I had to make sure they were going to be in town. I also insisted on an assurance they would not spill the beans before the event.

Aside from worries about the iceberg breaking up, Shrek falling off, the weather, etc, we were concerned the SPCA might take a dim view of shearing Shrek 100 kilometres off the coast of New Zealand on an iceberg. We were also worried Biosecurity New Zealand might call a halt on grounds that we could carry a foreign body back to shore.

There was a leak, as it happened. It could have come from anywhere because quite a few were involved, but it was easily plugged. Just as Shrek was being led to the helicopter to depart, Graeme Gale from Helicopters Otago received a call from the SPCA asking if he was taking Shrek out to an iceberg to shear him.

'No,' Graeme replied truthfully before hanging up.

He wasn't, and he didn't. It was Richard 'Hannibal' Hayes, from Te Anau, who flew Shrek to the iceberg.

And the result . . . Shrektacular!

National news, international news, people all around the world were talking again about the hermit sheep from New Zealand. He was in hot demand as a celebrity guest and the money continued to roll in for Cure Kids.

Other woolly sheep have surfaced since and have been compared with Shrek. They have had fleeting moments in the local media but that is all. Shrek is unique. He was at the right place, at the right time, found by the right shepherd, and taken under the right wing.

I am completely convinced that you could never plan nor buy this sort of publicity, this sort of success. It was good luck or good timing — or most likely just good alignment in the cosmos — which made Shrek a star.

As Jimmy shears Shrek, another berg floats close by.

Shrek on the huge rug branded with the Fernmark emblem, provided courtesy of his strong wool cousins.

Very relieved to be on our way back to the mainland.

This could so easily have been our last interview.

The helicopters hover on full power, poised to take off at any sign of the iceberg breaking up.

The Life of Shrek

You can't trust an iceberg

Above: Majestic but fragile pieces of Mother Nature. It's hard to imagine that the section we were standing on would be gone within a few hours of shearing Shrek. In hindsight, it wasn't one of my better ideas. A great experience, but a close call.

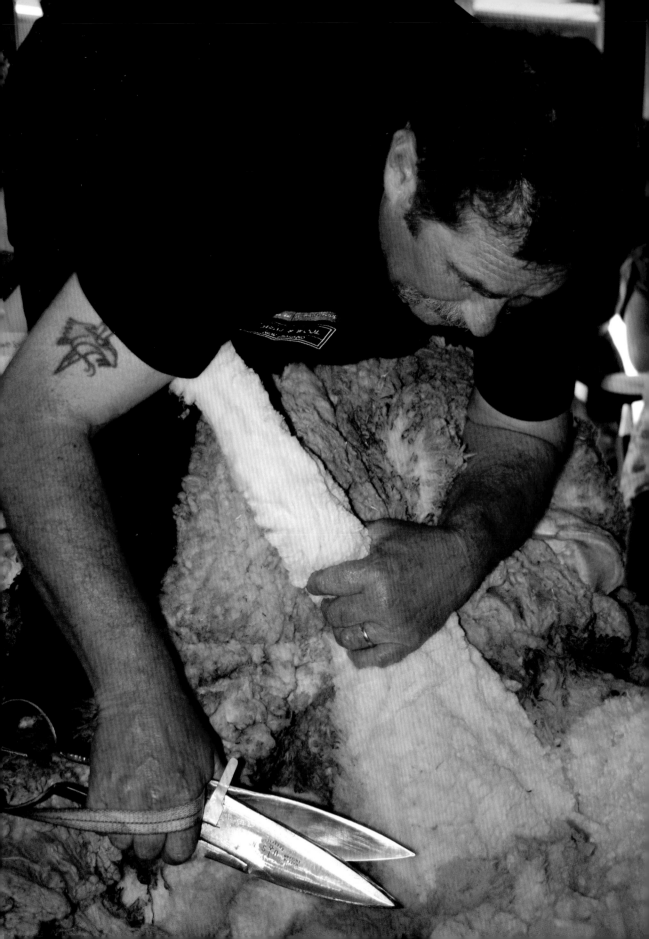

Chapter 8

Sky Tower Shearing

For the next two years Shrek continued his charity work, giving huge pleasure to many New Zealanders and raising lots more money for Cure Kids. He built up his Airpoints flying around New Zealand and was, in 2008, four years after being found at the top of Bendigo, still in hot demand.

Shrek never seemed to tire of the limelight, but it had been a long four years on the road and my long-suffering family was a bit over the whole Shrek thing. By now Shrek was 12, twice as old as any other Bendigo wether. Normally our wethers would be sold to the freezing works or to a down-country farmer by the age of six. As far as I know, no sheep has ever lived as long as Shrek.

Thanks to the bizarre turn of events, Shrek had led a charmed life but he was starting to show his age, moving more slowly and tiring more quickly. He was due to be shorn again so we decided to take the opportunity to announce his retirement from the national circuit. If required he would be available to make special guest appearances, but otherwise he would live out his days in the Bendigo ram shed, no doubt receiving yet more visitors and the usual tender loving care.

This final shearing needed to end Shrek's career in style. The top of Mt Cook, New Zealand's highest mountain, seemed the ultimate and most logical location, because Shrek was the king of New Zealand sheep. There had been several other publicity stunts on the mountain but they had very nearly ended in disaster.

At 12,000 feet, Mt Cook is an extremely inhospitable place. Helicopter pilots are only able to fly there for short bursts because of the lack of oxygen at that altitude. The last thing Cure Kids needed was a disaster. The New Zealand public — a nation of animal lovers — probably wouldn't have appreciated it either.

But I still wanted to satisfy my curiosity before canning the idea completely so I decided to do a reconnaissance trip with Dick Deaker. Dick was a pioneer from the wild deer-recovery days and still hunts with a Hughes 500 jet helicopter

Left: Billy Michelle blade shears Shrek at altitude, on the 51st floor of the Sky Tower.

Sky Tower Shearing **139**

in Fiordland. He is one of New Zealand's most experienced pilots, so I felt quite safe with him.

We flew up to the base flat at 3000 metres and looked up at the razor-sharp top ridge another 600 metres above. It was the most mongrel piece of rock I have ever seen. I am sure Shrek would not have been fazed about it as long as I was with him. But frankly I found just flying close to the summit and seeing the steep drop of thousands of metres one of the most spooky things I have ever done. I quickly agreed with Cure Kids. It was time for plan B!

That's when they came up with the idea of taking Shrek to New Zealand's biggest city, Auckland, to shear him at the top of the Sky Tower, New Zealand's tallest building. I loved the idea. Unlike an iceberg or a mountain, it would be a safe location and would not endanger the sanity of everyone involved! We could invite children along to watch the big event too.

I also wanted all the elderly people in retirement homes, patients in hospitals and the rest of New Zealand to have the opportunity to see Shrek being shorn. 'No problem! I'll arrange TV One's *Close Up* programme to come along,' said Josie.

Yet again Qantas got in behind us, agreeing to fly Shrek to Auckland for free. Accor Hotels provided accommodation for Josie, my daughter Christina, my brother Bob and me. They couldn't quite stretch to accommodating Shrek so he stayed with friends of mine in Parnell. Their Audi was left on the street and their garage was turned into a House of Shrek for the night. Sky City was happy to provide the 51st floor of the tower as the venue for the shearing. We were set!

My other concern was how well Shrek would travel. I thought he might be a bit shaky on his legs after being stuck in his crate for the 1 hour 40 minute flight from Queenstown. So, as I looked out of the window of the 737 after we'd landed at Auckland, my heart stopped for a few seconds. A large contingent of media with cameras was surrounding the arrival hall as Shrek's crate was being lifted sideways out of the aircraft's hold. Thankfully the airport crew were fabulous and I was allowed to go out the back to prepare him for his fans.

Much to my relief, as soon as Shrek saw the crowd, the old campaigner immediately put on his best public persona — like a racehorse going out of the birdcage onto the racetrack.

After greeting his fans, Shrek and his human entourage left the airport in a yellow stretch Hummerzine. He didn't seem to be very impressed with the glass

floor lit with psychedelic purple and orange disco-style lighting. You could almost read Shrek's thoughts, 'People have strange habits.' Back in his own shed, Shrek had always preferred listening to classical music on Radio New Zealand *Concert* and would become quite agitated with local DJs and their headbanging music.

We were headed to Shrek's pad at Parnell, but first I thought we'd make an impromptu visit to the upmarket Viaduct Basin down on Auckland's waterfront in the central business district. It was like the visit to Kirkcaldie & Stains department store in Wellington all over again. Shoppers and restaurant-goers looked on in amazement as two kids led a sheep in a red coat around the place. Then Bob and I took Shrek into the Cowboy bar for a beer.

Having seen the pleasure Shrek gives children, I really wanted to take Shrek to the Starship hospital. But times had changed and the powers that be wouldn't allow it. I couldn't believe we were being stopped from putting a smile on the faces of kids who really needed a treat. It was a shame but the best we could do was visit Ronald McDonald House without Shrek to speak to the families of the children and give them Shrek books and souvenir staples of wool.

Finally it was time to collect Shrek from Parnell in a black stretch Hummerzine and whisk him away celebrity-style to the Sky Tower. Crowds of children were there to greet him. We couldn't move when we arrived and people were pushing, trying to get photos, so we had to really fight our way into the tower for the shearing.

Shrek had no issues with the ride up in the glass lift looking out over Auckland

Above: Kids swarm to Shrek wherever he goes. Come to think of it, so do the adults!

city, but I can't say I felt the same. I have been in some tricky spots in the high country but seeing the city disappear below my feet was unnerving. But the show must go on, so I quietly turned to face the building as we scaled those 51 floors!

The official leader of the party was 12-year-old Selwyn Collins. Earlier that year his younger brother Scott had been given a 'Ticket to Hope' and he'd spent a weekend in Queenstown with his parents. However, sadly, the animal-mad boy had since passed away — so the shearing was dedicated to Scott and his family.

By now Billy Michelle, a champion blade shearer, was very nervous about shearing Shrek, even though he had won many national shearing titles. I was also a bit nervous about how Shrek would adjust to being 10–11 kilograms lighter. I expected him to feel a bit shaky, so we had done a 'dry run' at Bendigo. He seemed to be okay about being tipped over on his back, so we just crossed our fingers.

As it turned out, the shearing went without a hitch and in 40 minutes it was all over. When Billy finished the job he was very relieved to say, 'I now present you with the new Shrek!' It is amazing how the power of Shrek could put so much pressure on a gun shearer who had shorn tens of thousands of sheep over the years.

Billy was the third shearer to enter Shrek's hall of fame. First there had been Peter Casserly, who had shorn him in front of the world on the *Holmes* show. Then Jimmy Barnett had shorn him on the iceberg floating past New Zealand. And now Billy Michelle had shorn him at the top of the Sky Tower on national TV. What more could Cure Kids and Shrek's New Zealand fans wish for?

For his swansong, I thought it would be fabulous if Shrek could fly home in style. Shrek's friend, businessman Andy Low, owned a private jet — and when I asked him whether it might be possible to borrow his plane to fly back to Wanaka, the answer was instant: 'Not a problem. It will be waiting at Auckland airport for you both.'

Very soon after take-off Shrek was sound asleep. Little did he know that the Low Corporation is one of New Zealand's biggest meat processors. Shrek's story was so powerful it had earned the company's respect, enabling him to fly from one end of the country to the other in a private jet, free of charge.

My son Daniel was waiting at Wanaka with his friend Gus and a Jet 500 helicopter to take Shrek straight to Bendigo, where he happily tucked into his evening meal of oats only two hours after leaving Auckland.

Shrek was part of our family and probably became the most spoilt member!

Cage and Billy relaxing before the big event.

Seat belt on, scorching through the southern skies toward Wanaka with Hawke's Bay businessman Graeme Lowe.

Matt Chisholm provides more great media coverage for Shrek and his favourite charity, Cure Kids.

Looking up at the place where Shrek was about to be shorn.

On the way to the tallest man-made structure in New Zealand.

The Life of Shrek
Off to the Sky Tower

Above: Mount Aspiring — another Kiwi icon.   Sky Tower Shearing **147**

Above: Lake Dunstan lies quietly at the foot of Bendigo Station.

Chapter 9

Shrek's Home at Bendigo Station

Bendigo first entered the national consciousness back in the 1860s when gold was discovered up in the barren and inhospitable gullies of the Dunstan Mountains. During the gold rush days Bendigo was part of the great Morven Hills pastoral run, a huge property of approximately 162,000 hectares covering the Lindis and Tarras area. But by the time the goldminers left Bendigo, Morven Hills had been broken up into many smaller high country runs including what is now Bendigo Station, home of Shrek.

I have always had a love and fascination for the merino, whose heritage dates back to 2000 BC and which, during the early industralisation of the world, were the prized possessions of kings and queens. The fibre they produce is natural and sustainable and the garments woven from it are worn by babies, sportsmen and the most beautiful women in the world.

Merinos are truly remarkable creatures in every respect and have been regarded as the king of all sheep breeds since the colonisation of New Zealand over 150 years ago. They make up only 3 per cent of the 30-odd million sheep in New Zealand. And of that elite group, only one has ever attracted world fame and become a celebrity. His name is Shrek.

If Shrek was to return to the hills and high country of Bendigo, he would still exhibit the

Shrek doesn't see himself as a sheep, instead preferring to be on his own and with human company, especially children.

unique traits of other merinos in the way he moves, feeds and interacts with the rugged environment around him. The only difference today is that Shrek doesn't see himself as a sheep, instead preferring to be on his own and with human company, especially children.

Merinos are gentle animals that generally live in the high country, so tourists seldom see them. They produce a soft fibre covered in a thin film of lanolin to

protect it from the harsh environment they live in. As the fibre grows on the back of the animal, Mother Nature creates crimps in it. The frequency and number of crimps per centimetre is genetically linked to generations of human influence in creating types that best suit the end textile product. For example, a superfine merino or Saxon merino will produce many more crimps and the fibre will be woven into lightweight fabrics, such as merino suits and women's fashion wear. These wools generally range from 15 to 16 microns, a micron being a precise measurement of the thickness of the fibre.

Shrek has a micron of 19.8 and his fleece would normally be used for fine knitted fabrics that companies such as Icebreaker have become famous for. It is a fitting tribute to his kinfolk that Shrek always wears his red coat made by Icebreaker.

I always envy merinos as they generally live above

Top: Heather's hen lays as Shrek has a bite to eat. **Above:** Shrek's ear-tag, 2835, that he has carried all his life.

what I call worry level in the high country; they move around quietly, unless a dog turns up; and they take time to select their preferred plants for feeding. From early morning they will spread out over the hill country, quietly grazing between the tussocks, and in the evening will quietly drift back together, generally in groups on high knobs.

Although New Zealand is a very safe country and has no predators, such as lions, tigers, coyotes, wolves or snakes, merinos still hold in their genetics from early European days survival traits similar to humans'. In early times the safest place was on top of a hill or in large groups. So when musterers turn up with dogs barking, the merinos naturally start moving or running uphill and gather into mobs for safety reasons.

The extreme example of this is mustering ewes with their young lambs. The lambs have never seen a dog in their lives before but will follow their mums down a hill, with men and dogs behind, until they get to a gate on a fenceline. If mum goes through, the lamb will follow. But if mum is suspicious of going through the gate this immediately sets off alarm bells throughout the flock. The experienced musterer will quietly pull back with the dogs and wait for a ewe to

Above: With his cover off, Shrek gets some much needed rest on his sun deck after his big birthday celebrations.

finally gain the confidence to go through the gate.

It is a very fine line and I don't know how many times I have seen an inexperienced musterer's dogs, not under control, put too much pressure on the mob — then all hell breaks loose. For the lambs there is only one way out of a trapped situation and it is not through the gate, but back up the hill. Men and dogs become mere obstacles for the lambs to run past or jump over and this confusion and chaos is usually fuelled by men shouting and chasing their dogs to try and give them a hiding for causing the problem. Ninety-nine times out of a hundred it is the man's fault, and if the dog has had a hiding before, he will try and hide in the middle of the mob, which causes even greater chaos.

Putting the odd clash between the inexperienced musterer and the merino aside, moving stock with good shepherds and dogs around you would have to be one of my greatest enjoyments as a merino farmer. The tranquillity and silence of the high country is an environmental gem we take for granted.

Several years ago when I was heavily involved with helping set up new marketing opportunities for merino wool, an English manufacturer visited Bendigo. I took him up the hill to show him the view and was busy pointing out all the landmarks — Mt Aspiring, Lake Hawea, Mt Pisa, Lindis Pass and Mt Cook. And as I waffled on, he suddenly said, 'Could you just shut up for a minute?'

Bloody ungrateful Pom, I thought. How wrong I was!

'Can you hear that?' he asked. 'I have never experienced it in my life before.'

'What's that?' I said.

'Silence. The sound of silence.'

Above: The morning sun moves over the Bendigo paddocks as Shrek rises, looking out at another day in paradise.

It was a lasting emotional memory for that manufacturer from busy industrial England, and the company become one of our best customers. It also left me with a determination to protect not only our landscape in New Zealand but the tranquillity of our environment. Shrek had that well worked out when he chose to live at over 5000 feet.

In 2008 I got a call from the producers of New Zealand's rural TV show *Country Calendar*. Would I be interested in them doing a programme on Bendigo Station, home of Shrek? *Country Calendar* is New Zealand's longest-running TV programme and there have been huge protests whenever TVNZ has proposed cutting the show, the management mistakenly thinking New Zealanders are no longer interested in rural life.

Heather and I didn't have a problem with their request, so the film crew duly arrived. The show was very well received and made that year's *Best of Country Calendar* collection. It also rescreened in 2010 in the show which celebrated

Above: Grandchildren Olly and Lucy unveil the Paul Dibble bronze to commemorate 100 years of Bendigo Station.

40 years of *Country Calendar*.

New Zealand is also a nation of readers and we have a huge appetite for books about ourselves. So when Jenny Hellen, the Deputy Publishing Director at Random House in Auckland, saw the *Country Calendar* programme, she recognised another bestseller in the making.

The book would focus on Shrek — the darling of the international media and much-loved national icon. But like the *Country Calendar* programme, it would also tell the rest of the Bendigo story from its early days as part of a giant Malvern Hills pastoral run through to its development as a sheep station and home of award-winning Pinot Noir vineyards. Bendigo's stunning landscapes would also be a huge selling point.

Bendigo Station was due to celebrate its 100-year anniversary and Heather and I had been thinking about a book. But having no experience at all in publishing, we had little idea how we would go about it. Heather wasn't interested in writing and I had never learnt to spell, having failed my School Certificate exams and been asked not to come back to Waitaki Boys the next year. I didn't see it as any great tragedy at the time because as a teenager I was more interested in hunting, riding rodeo and spending time in my Mark I Zephyr.

Jenny assured me that writing a book wouldn't be too hard. The Bendigo story was a good one and I would have the support of a professional co-author to help get the words down on paper. I agreed, but weeks turned into months and soon it was 2009. I was busy and not a lot happened. Jenny was on my case to start writing. She needed the manuscript by the end of May for it to be in the shops for Christmas.

With less than two months until the deadline I was forced into action. There is always something happening at Bendigo, so I resorted to getting up and writing in the

There is always something happening at Bendigo, so I resorted to getting up and writing in the early hours when there were no interruptions.

early hours when there were no interruptions. After many broken nights the manuscript for *Dust to Gold: The inspiring story of Bendigo Station, home of Shrek* was written — much to my family's relief.

There are over 350 photos in *Dust to Gold* and at least of half of them were taken by Stephen Jaquiery. Quick to smile, Stephen has a great but subtle sense of humour — he tells people he works for John Perriam and takes photos for the

Above: Shrek looks on as Budge eyeballs and quietly works Heather's hens. Just another day at home for Shrek.

Otago Daily Times on the side. In actual fact he is the Illustrations Editor for the paper and occasionally slips his collar to join Shrek and me on our latest project. He won't admit it, but he loves pushing the boundaries, capturing people and everything that is different about New Zealand.

Stephen lives with his wife Jane and daughter Phoebe in Dunedin but I am absolutely sure he sleeps with his camera. It intrigues me that Jane is also a photographer, which must make for interesting pillow talk when the lights go down.

Stephen is an amazing photographer and has that X-factor that propelled Shrek to stardom. It would never have happened if Stephen hadn't pushed the shutter at that exact split second, capturing an image that turned Shrek from an ordinary — albeit very woolly — sheep, into a creature that captured the world's imagination.

The worst thing you can do is to tell Stephen how he should take a photo or even make a suggestion, because he is a genuine artist.

Once we arrive at a place where we want to photograph Shrek, patience becomes the most important virtue. Stephen just keeps snooping around, looking and waiting for the right moment.

Driving to a photo shoot, I might say, 'That looks like a great shot, Stephen.' He usually just looks very unimpressed and ignores my comment, but over the years I've learnt reverse psychology works well. Just the other day we were driving through the Mackenzie Basin, a place of extraordinary natural beauty.

Capturing an image that turned Shrek from an ordinary — albeit very woolly — sheep, into a creature that captured the world's imagination.

'Telecom are bloody environmental vandals,' I said, referring to power poles marching out into the wide open spaces like a row of soldiers. 'Stop,' he replied and spent the next 10 minutes taking photographs of them. He certainly has a wonderful gift. Shrek has made the most of it and both Stephen and Shrek have been an inspiration to New Zealanders. I count myself very fortunate to have been part of their journey.

Even once the manuscript was written and the photos were taken, I found there was still an awful lot of work to do to produce the final product. Heather and I took a short holiday to Rarotonga after the manuscript was written to escape the cold Tarras fog for a week. She reckoned it was the only way to get me to stop working, but I took the 'final' manuscript along and kept coming up with new stories to add! Heather reckoned it was like having 'Camilla' on holiday — there was her, me and the manuscript!

Random House is a well-oiled book marketing machine and, based on forward sales to booksellers, *Dust to Gold* had to be reprinted before it hit the shops, which is pretty rare in New Zealand. Within three weeks it went to number one in New Zealand adult non-fiction.

I regard myself as a high country tussock jumper rather than an author so I was quite stunned. To drive sales, publicist Jennifer Balle from Random organised a very full schedule of media interviews and public speaking engagements to promote the book. She was very efficient and punctual to the point of almost driving me insane! We'd often arrive early at speaking engagements and I'd end up walking around a rugby field or car park in my merino suit for half an hour, killing time. I soon discovered why she insisted on being so punctual. It was a bit of a culture shock to discover city people were always sitting ready to hear my presentation at the advertised time. In the country, people only start arriving at the advertised time and talk with each other before taking a seat. So you are forgiven, Jennifer!

Shrek came out of retirement to make a trip to Winton Library, which was full of children who had

Above: Like soldiers, this row of power poles marches in a line across the majestic Mackenzie Basin, named after the infamous sheep thief, James Mackenzie.

bused in from all over Southland. Winton is a three-hour drive from Bendigo, so Jennifer had insisted on another early start. Noticing I looked bleary eyed she suddenly said, 'John, you are looking tired! Do you think we should pull in to the next motel so you can have a power nap?'

Although I am just a farm boy and Jennifer is a sophisticated city girl this saying got my attention instantly. Musterers have been known to curl up under a tussock for a short kip but I'd never heard the term 'power nap' before. I politely declined and we got to Winton early.

Another time, Jennifer booked us into a motel on the outskirts of Feilding so we could get an early start to our next engagement. A large number of trucks were stopped there, but I never gave it a second thought at the time. Jennifer arranged to knock on my door, unit 7, at 5 am. I knew it was far too early but didn't argue.

So, next morning at exactly one minute to 5, I heard 'knock, knock' on my door. 'Blast,' I thought. 'I will stay quiet and read the paper for half an hour.'

Not getting any confirmation that I had heard the knock, Jennifer started to panic. Perhaps she was mistaken and I was staying in unit 17, not unit 7, she thought. So down the row of units she went and knocked on number 17. This time she got a

Above: These children in Winton hadn't seen a sheep like Shrek before. 'Are you for real?' they said, patting him to make sure.

response. A big truckie dressed only in his jocks flung open the door.

A slightly flustered Jennifer apologised profusely and began to explain she had the wrong unit. But the truckie disagreed and beamed: 'You can knock on my door anytime. You've made my day. Come on in.' Jennifer laughs about it now and we have since reached an understanding about not arriving early.

Public speaking is a great fear of many people. As a young man I could never have stood on a public platform and strung two words together without my mind going blank. Like many young people in New Zealand, I was very insecure. Alcohol was the only thing that gave me a false confidence. But then I found Heather on an agricultural exchange scheme in Canada. From a young age she had an air of authority and her presence commanded respect — all the qualities I lacked.

Heather didn't change me overnight, and I often wonder at the incredible challenge she took on. But change did come slowly — though occasionally the power of the dram still took over.

But today I enjoy telling the stories and people love hearing them. People are hungry for a good true New Zealand success story, even though many can't help themselves from indulging in the national pastime of knocking the tall poppy. It has also become very obvious to me that a lot of people have a secret ambition to write a book, as it has a way of immortalising the subject — in this case the quirky but wonderful story of Shrek, an old merino sheep.

So how did a high country tussock jumper manage to write a New Zealand best-seller? The answer is quite simple. First he fell in love with the subject — the high country and the people and animals that live there. Second, he built the right team around himself.

As a complete novice of an author I would never have put pen to paper without mentors and a respected retail publisher. The photographer, Stephen Jaquiery; my assistant writer, Robin Major; my publisher, Jenny Hellen, and her editorial team; and Jennifer Balle, my publicist, were all essential to the success of *Dust to Gold*. I couldn't have done it on my own. And besides, working as part of a team is so much more rewarding than being a loner. Just ask Shrek!

Grahame Sydney Paints Shrek's Rock

I have had the great privilege to get to know painter Grahame Sydney. His magnificent paintings of Central Otago landscapes are collected by the likes of Elton John, Nelson Mandela and Sam Neill.

Years ago I helped Syd find a small cottage at Mt Pisa Station, opposite Bendigo, where he could set up and paint.

'Perhaps you could paint something of Bendigo one day, Grahame,' I said.

'Okay,' Syd said and he did keep his word.

I couldn't believe it when I saw the painting, destined to become one of his most famous art collection pieces. Like Stephen, Syd had done it his way, from the perspective of inside a round concrete tank house with a very small window, facing Bendigo. From this position he had painted a little framed landscape of the exact place where Shrek was to be found years later. This was the year before Shrek even thought of going AWOL. Freakish! Bendigo is a vast landscape and I am sure Syd was taking the mickey out of the fact that it was a very large station.

The Killing House by Grahame Sydney. The view out the window looking across from Mt Pisa points at Shrek's cave, even though the painting predates the arrival of Shrek. This extraordinary painting by Grahame resonates well with Shrek's story. It's something Shrek doesn't like to think about, but for centuries people depended on meat for survival, hence the dark and deathly look inside the tank. But the little window suggests hope and possibility for the future. I believe Shrek has provided that hopeful ray of light to so many children and people around New Zealand, so it is fitting that the frame miraculously happens to be the exact place where he was found.

Collection, Manawatu Art Gallery, Palmerston North.

Heather, the Mother of Shrek.

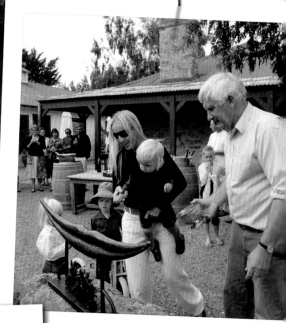

Sarah, holding Max, and me on a historic day for Bendigo Station, 28 February 2010.

Heather and me, with the newest member of our family at the time, Shrek.

Stewart with Lucy, Olly and friends, unveiling the Paul Dibble bronze as we celebrate 100 years at Bendigo.

Daniel, Pip and Lucy meet Shrek for the first time.

The Life of Shrek

With the family

Above: The 45th Parallel sign in front of Lake Dunstan and Northburn Station. The 45th Parallel marks a theoretical halfway point between the equator and the South Pole at a latitude of 45 degrees south. The imaginary line runs right through Bendigo and within metres of Shrek's cave.

Chapter 10

The Guy Who Fenced Shrek's Block

Shrek's block high up on Bendigo was fenced by the hard case character Willy Wong, who lives not far from the homestead up the Ardgour Valley. His real name is Bill Cowie but he looks a bit Chinese and was given his nickname many years ago when he dressed up as a Chinese gold miner for a school play.

Wong has played a huge part in the development of Bendigo Station, erecting virtually every fence on the place — giving us the ability to move stock according to the seasons, limiting grazing of environmentally sensitive areas and retiring other areas completely.

The New Zealand high country is not an easy place to fence and Bendigo is particularly challenging, being littered with rocky canyons and valleys. But as far as Wong is concerned, the steeper a rocky canyon, the bigger the challenge and the more he enjoys his job.

During his fencing career he has survived close to 30 major accidents and has broken nearly every bone in his body in the process. He is now virtually completely deaf due to his favourite pastime of using explosives with as short a fuse as possible to blow fencepost holes in the rock. His yard is littered with wrecked Land-Rovers and machinery, each one telling a story of a close call or near miss.

But largely thanks to Wong's efforts Bendigo is now fenced into approximately 30, mainly hill, blocks. Each has been given a name, such as Wong's block — one of the most rugged he fenced — and Shrek's block directly above it, where Shrek was found.

The block of land now known as Shrek's block was fenced off from the lower oversown land to separate

Left and above: Landscaping is in the eye of the beholder. 'One man's junk is another man's treasure,' Billy Wong says.

conservation land from freehold land. Shrek wasn't aware of this until winter set in and he found the new fence barred his way. To date, over 40 per cent of the South Island high country has been turned into public conservation parks and merinos have been denied the right of access.

Wong had considerable trouble fencing Shrek's block. He rolled his favourite old Land-Rover into a gully and lost a tractor-load of fencing gear 300 metres down into the Devil's Canyon. A lot of explosive gelignite was used and for weeks we could hear the blasts echoing around Bendigo hills and the Upper Clutha basin.

Wong's philosophy is that every time he rolls a Land-Rover down into a gully, he will retrieve what remains to help restore other vehicles — so he never needs to buy a new one. He is right to a certain degree. Some parts do survive many complete write-offs but in a lot of situations they are faulty and the cause of the next catastrophe. Wong doesn't believe in insurance, or many other things in life other people believe are essential.

Thirty years ago, when Heather and I arrived at Bendigo, my first sight of Wong was high up in the hill country. We heard the sound of an old helicopter coming over the brow of a hill. It was midwinter and we were trying to muster in the snow. Over the chopper went, Wong standing outside the helicopter with one foot on

Above: Wong and his favourite foxie.

the skid, holding on to a deer antler with one hand and the helicopter with the other. Wong has always been such a colourful character and has an enjoyable dry sense of wit and humour, he is considered part of our family at Bendigo.

Wong also has a great love of animals — birds, horses, dogs, turkeys, hens, peacocks — you name it. All his pets have names too. His cat is called Joe Rokocoko, after the All Black winger. The Jack Russells are called Gorbachev after the Russian president, Spotty Bum, Super Cooper, Houchy Poochy, The Deacon, Bum Hockle Stead, and so on. Wong also loves to see his animals multiply with no particular breeding objective in mind, much to the amazement of many farming neighbours.

Wong is a man of few words and his four boys are a chip off the old block. One day Max Broadmore was helping Wong, along with his boys, nicknamed Grumpy and Lindis (named after the river that ran past his house in the Ardgour). They came off the hill late in the day in the old unregistered Bedford truck and ran the gauntlet up the highway, hoping not to run into a traffic officer.

Max was driving as they came to the busy state highway. Grumpy was sitting in the far left side of the cab so Max asked him: 'Are there any cars coming, Grumpy?'

To which Grumpy, in his drawn out way, replied, 'No . . .'

Max let the clutch out and the old Bedford lurched out onto the highway. Then Grumpy, quite disturbed, said: 'But there is a big bus, Max.'

> *Wong has always been such a colourful character and has an enjoyable dry sense of wit and humour, he is considered part of our family at Bendigo.*

Max doesn't know to this day how the bus missed them! It was the closest call of his life.

Wong may be an expert in the high country fencing game, but unfortunately he has not been so successful in matters of the heart. He and his wife Beverly parted company while he was working on a fence at Bendigo. When he found out she had left him for another man, he was determined to throttle the guy. Somehow, at 3 am, I managed to calm him down and make him see sense before any damage was done.

Wong wasn't partial to being a bachelor. So before long he spotted an advert for mail-order brides from Asia and sent off his money, much to the horror of the

local ladies. Heather couldn't get her mind around this idea, even though she and Wong had a great rapport and she even offered the use of Bendigo's historic homestead and grounds for his wedding if it ever came to that.

Wong's house up the Ardgour Valley near Bendigo wasn't exactly palatial, as Wong had openly stated to the nation on *Country Calendar*. One man's junk is another man's treasure, so the build-up of everything imaginable around his house turned Wong's abode into a kind of treasure trove. Chooks laid in old hay bailers and foxy dogs played and mated in old Land-Rovers.

Heather decided that the situation would be impossible for some poor unsuspecting Asian woman and again talked to Wong about rethinking his decision, but she couldn't change his mind. Soon Connie was on her way to a new life in New Zealand along with Wong, his treasures and pets.

Wong had sent Connie a photo taken from his house of the magnificent million-dollar views of Dunstan Mountains and Lindis Pass lined with autumn golden willows. She never saw the actual house until she arrived.

Fortunately Connie did develop a very soft spot for Wong and they were duly married at Bendigo. Unfortunately the marriage didn't last too many years. Wong was very upset because she claimed half of his hens as part of the separation settlement. That was the last straw for Wong and now he prefers the company of his mates, fox terriers, turkeys, horses and pigs.

Above: The tranquil Ardgour Valley is home to Billy Wong and others in the small Tarras community.

Fiona Rowley, a great lady of the high country who bonded with Shrek immediately.

Ginny Rutledge and Kirsty Hewitt, either side of a very handsome sheep.

Two local characters, P.L.Anderson and Brandy.

The Wanaka Stars in Your Eyes singers, known to us as the Bendigo Bandits, who sung to fundraise for cancer. Bex Murray (centre) and Paul Tamati (top right) also sung at a high-tea farewell concert for Heather at Bendigo.

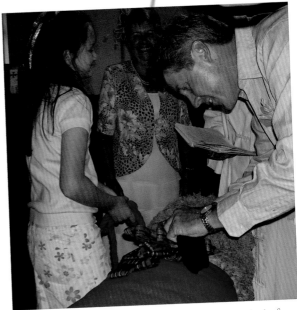

People who know Shrek definitely come to think of him as a friend. At Zimbabwean couple Duncan and Janie Cramp's wedding he was even the best man! Megan Topping is the bridesmaid.

The red-headed Gnome, telling yet another joke, inside this restored hut at Nine Mile Historic Reserve.

The Life of Shrek

The locals

Chapter 11

The House of Shrek

Shrek must surely be the only sheep in New Zealand to have his own house. Known as the House of Shrek, it was originally built to display stud pedigree rams and ewes, along with their fleece wool and prized show ribbons and trophies.

But since the day Shrek was dumped in the ram shed as a common woolly wether it has remained solely his as we turned our efforts at Bendigo away from showing at A&P Shows towards raising funds for Cure Kids.

Shrek's complex, complete with sun deck, is approximately one metre off the ground. The main living area is constructed with grating on the floor, very high ceilings and a roof that is totally lined. This provides a cool environment during the hot Central Otago summer and warmth during the winter.

He has a mezzanine floor and large wall shutters that can be opened or shut depending on the conditions. His foyer contains large displays of his Bendigo cousins competing at shows and people, musterers and family who have been involved over the years. On the other walls are displays of show ribbons, proudly won over the years.

Large sliding doors at each end of his complex control the risk of a stray dog getting in to harm him. So, at Bendigo, Shrek lives in a controlled and secure environment, a little like a gated community in the city. He has a radio quietly playing classical music. He is very relaxed in this environment but gets quite agitated if he hears headbanging music in the woolshed. If we opened the gate from his little outside grazing pen to allow him to go freely and join other sheep, he wouldn't go!

The night Shrek was shorn in front of the world, a Japanese film crew stayed in his complex as part of a documentary that was broadcast to over a third of their nation. The footage showed that he never slept, but instead walked around — for the first time in years being able to see everything around him. Then the crew noticed he was shivering, even with his red coat on, and they became very concerned, knocking on our door at 3 am.

'Mr John? Shrek, he very cold, you come see.'

It was a chilly autumn night and the cold air was rolling off the hills around our homestead and Shrek's complex. Despite the hour I was pleased they'd woken me and when I looked at Shrek he didn't seem happy. Whether it was the shock of the shearing and seeing Paul Holmes for the first time or the cold, we weren't going to take any chances.

Heather had one of the offices set up for her Suprino fashion business, but this was an emergency, so at 3.30 am all Heather's cabinets, folders and desks were thrown out, the big heater was turned on and straw spread over the floor for Shrek to sleep on. Shrek seemed settled for the rest of the night, so we all went back to bed. The Japanese film crew were very happy and next day the papers ran the news item: 'Shrek Takes Over Bendigo Office'.

At 4.30 am our good photographer Stephen Jaquiery and Dave Cannan, of the *Otago Daily Times*, had finally finished their bottle of Scotch before retiring to the shearers' quarters for some sleep. For whatever reason, they decided to check Shrek and noticed a small end of poly twine hanging from the side of his mouth. Stephen started to pull it and, to his horror, it kept coming and coming out of his mouth and stomach — many, many metres of it. How Shrek didn't die within a few hours of shearing is another miracle; and why he ate all of the poly twine from the straw bales he could find is a mystery. In the rush to move all the office furniture and lay the straw, removing the twine from the straw bales had been overlooked in the dead of the night.

Above: Sunrise over Shrek's house at Bendigo.   The House of Shrek **181**

Shrek only stayed in Heather's office for one night. Heather was pleased to have her office back, although within a short time she had to move again. A sign, 'Shrek's Office', was put on the door and inside were displayed his many news clippings, photos, cartoons and of course what remained of his super-long prized fleece after the rest was used for souvenirs.

For the days and weeks that followed, the House of Shrek was Shrek's safe haven from the intense media and public interest. It may sound strange but we seriously looked at ways to fit locks and security on his complex, because the media said he was worth hundreds of thousands. One American actually made a ridiculous offer that I refused. We even approached insurance companies to look at insuring Shrek from the unthinkable, but at the end of the day realised he really was only a worthless old wether. His story was what made him valuable and that was something nobody could steal or destroy.

One night a whacky TV programme called *Eating Media Lunch* showed Shrek

Above: Many thousands of children have visited Shrek at home over the years. He loves playing and has great patience with them all.

being slaughtered and hung up with his red cover on. The next scene was diners eating lamb cutlets. After that our phone went crazy with people from all over New Zealand ringing until 3 am inquiring about Shrek's welfare. They were horrified by the show and it took quite a lot of media coverage to convince the public it was a spoof.

The ram shed was for Shrek's exclusive use but in September 2004 Ann found a newborn bull calf deserted and desperately hanging on to life in the nearby poplar tree paddock. She brought it down and asked if she could put it in Shrek's house overnight. The calf's mother was nowhere to be seen and this big leggy brown creature lay on the grating, gasping and occasionally giving a kick.

Shrek wasn't overly sure about having a visitor to stay but it needed help or would be dead in the morning. After giving it penicillin and colostrum milk, Ann went home. I

At first Shrek seemed to resent the calf taking up residence in his place, but over the months they became very good mates.

thought it was a goner so was absolutely amazed the next morning when the calf was not only alive but trying to struggle to its feet. During the morning it finally got to its feet but was very unsteady, staggering around.

At first Shrek seemed to resent the calf taking up residence in his place, but over the months they became very good mates, playing and butting each other up and down the ramp of the shed. They shared their feed in the morning and at night, developing a special relationship.

At the tender age of three months, the calf, now named Herman, was put out in a paddock out the front of Shrek's complex. Shrek could watch him grazing from his balcony. A year later I decided Herman could come and have Christmas dinner with Shrek, and I gave them both a big bucket of chaff and oats. It was great to see them together again.

I popped outside for a moment to put the dogs away when suddenly I heard a huge commotion. Returning to Shrek's complex to see what was wrong I saw Shrek pinned up against the wall with all four legs off the ground. Herman was doing all he could to break every rib in Shrek's body.

Like many humans, greed had got the better of Herman and he had changed. Unfortunately Herman burned his bridges with me that day and he became a beef burger at McDonald's. I haven't told Ann yet and I am sure she won't be happy when she finds out what happened to her mate!

A few years ago Kaye Parker of Cure Kids wanted to give some visiting Irish children a treat so a visit to Shrek was arranged. We thought it might be a good time to take Shrek back into his cave high up on Bendigo as it was summer and there was no snow.

So off we went up to Devil's Creek, then on foot for an hour up through the speargrass and rocky faces. Shrek wasn't as fit as he used to be and I was worried about him having a heart attack on the mountain.

The kids had a great day and it was incredible on the way up to see Shrek walking in a row with the children, with no lead. At his cave Shrek looked around but didn't show any great interest in being back at his cave. He was very happy to set off back down the hill to his house at the station with the kids.

Being on a main highway, Bendigo is not hard to find and since the day Shrek was found many people have simply come in off the road to visit Shrek, often without warning. This is sometimes difficult as we are a working farm but we always try to make people welcome. In the early days it all got a bit out of hand so after a while we requested that if possible people come in groups at pre-arranged times so I can be available to supervise and answer their questions.

Over the last six years, his highness has received visitors on a daily basis. For this reason he always wears his red-branded Cure Kids coat just in case. They come in busloads and, without exception, Shrek meets, greets and charms them, leaving a lasting emotional experience they'll never forget.

As groups of people enter his foyer Shrek will boldly walk up to greet the group, no matter how large or small. Some people become quite emotional and the sheer excitement and joy they get out of meeting the old celebrity is something that continues to amaze me.

Often the visitors have already visited the Bendigo goldfields and looked through the historic Bendigo homestead, but the highlight of their trip is always going next door to the House of Shrek to meet, see, touch and have their photo taken with his highness. And Shrek knows it!

Something I have grown to understand is what it is like becoming a slave to an iconic sheep. I think it could only happen in New Zealand.

Above: Shrek prepares himself for yet another onslaught of kids.   The House of Shrek **185**

186 Shrek: The story of a Kiwi icon

Above: The Hawkdun Range, Central Otago, at dusk.   The House of Shrek **187**

Chapter 12

Shrek's Pet Hate

Shrek is generally a very sociable character but he has one pet hate — dogs! In fact, I'd go so far as to say that as far as Shrek is concerned they are all evil and cannot be trusted, no matter how large or small. Obviously he has had a bad experience with them in his early years and many wannabe analysts hold the view this is why he went AWOL for five years.

Once when Shrek was leading the Waikaia pet parade, he spotted a Jack Russell in the crowd. The poor child trying to lead him behind the bagpiper was dragged into the crowd in pursuit! No one got hurt; but a later incident at Bendigo was more serious.

A family connected to the local Mud House Winery came to visit Shrek with their six-year-old girl. As they walked around his pen taking photos, Shrek seemed a little agitated, which I thought was quite strange. The little girl was carrying a soft little rag doll, but I didn't see why that would be the problem.

Then I noticed Shrek starting to follow the little girl around and, to my horror, out of the corner of my eye I saw him charge and flatten the little girl on the grating. Amongst the commotion and howling, he was trying to rake the rag doll away over to the corner of the house with his front feet and get it out the door.

The little girl was okay but, not surprisingly, her family never came back again to see Shrek. We later found out that a dog had played with the little girl's doll the day before. It all suddenly added up. Shrek's strong sense of smell and absolute hatred of dogs had caused him to have a brain explosion. For a few seconds hatred had overridden his compassion for young children.

The only dog Shrek has learnt to tolerate in his house is my daughter Christina's little terrier Mimi. She visits Shrek while Christina works in the next room on her fashion business. It is never long before the cat and mouse performance starts with Shrek trying to chase Mimi out of his space.

Mimi has learnt that if she quickly ducks in behind Shrek she is safe, but Shrek

still tries every trick in the book to headbutt or stomp the little dog. It has become a daily game with little Mimi always having the safe option of ducking under a rail, much to Shrek's annoyance. A dog's a dog in Shrek's book and it is incredible they are the only animal he doesn't like.

When our family had to spend a lot of time in Christchurch recently, taking Mimi for a walk through the suburbs became the daily ritual and a whole new experience unfolded. There was a lot to get used to. First there was the extendable lead that Mimi didn't want to know about. Then there were all the trucks and buses that she thought should give way to her. So off we would go — farm boy

Above: Christina's dog, Mimi. How could one little dog be so much trouble?

in Airtex shirt, moleskin trousers and RM Williams riding boots and scruffy little Mimi on a lead — we soon learnt we stood out like a sore toe.

The first thing we encountered was other people walking dogs of all shapes and sizes, carrying plastic bags and long extendable gadgets for picking up their excrement. Full of self-importance, Mimi piddled on every tree and strange doggy-smelling object and would try and interact with other dogs, for which she'd get the occasional snarl in return.

Then, as nature took over, she had a poo stop just as a very well-groomed lady with a very well-groomed poodle was coming the other way. She quickly summed up the situation — that I was straight off the farm — and said, 'Oh, I'm sorry, old chap. You must pick up all your dog's droppings.'

Without a plastic bag or what they called a 'pooper-scooper' it was a bit problematic as I wasn't going to put Mimi's business in my pocket. Once we got over these obstacles, however, Mimi had a marvellous time meeting and greeting other dogs, regardless of their size. As we walked past one house, a menacing pair of Rottweilers came tearing out of a driveway towards her. One bite and she would be turned into a feather duster. I must admit that the hair went up on the back of my neck too.

I found myself subconsciously reaching for the 12 gauge shotgun that sits behind the seat of the farm Toyota. My heart went out to defenceless people when confronted by in-timidating dogs.

The next day I thought we had everything under control. Mimi had relieved herself once out of sight behind a tree and we were walking along when we saw the same lady coming the other way again. Just as we were about to pass her to my horror I felt a sharp tug on the lead behind me: Mimi was about to relieve herself again.

I didn't want to allow this little white fluffy creature to embarrass me so kept walking.

I didn't want to allow this little white fluffy creature to embarrass me so kept walking. Mimi on the other hand had a strong will and wasn't going to give up, so I kept walking with Mimi dragging along, her back legs up off the ground.

Above: A long day during the autumn muster.

The next day I felt obliged to stop and apologise to the lady but when she learnt I was the father of Shrek, all was forgiven. Even back in the ram shed at Bendigo old Shrek was getting me off the hook in Christchurch!

I couldn't get over how the mannerisms of city dogs are so like their owners. Some were very friendly and laid-back, wanting to talk all day if you let them. Others would go past, nose in the air, with their poncy owner following along in similar fashion. One couple I met looked at scruffy little Mimi and said, 'And what is that?'

I immediately sensed the social importance of being seen with the right dog, just as some people like to be seen with the right people. So on the defence and distancing myself from the stigma Mimi brought, I said, 'Oh, this thing belongs to my daughter.'

The beautifully groomed dog gave Mimi the once over while I asked, 'And what breed is your dog?'

'Oh, Victoria is a Labradoodle, extremely well bred by Sir Charles.'

When I got back to the house I said, 'Christina, Mimi is going to have to get scrubbed up.' So in she went to the dog groomer for a trim and complete makeover that I think cost more than Mimi originally did, and so she was transformed into a city dog. I bought a pair of walking shoes and a Canterbury tracksuit that seemed socially acceptable, although the city never did take the farm out of the boy.

Putting Shrek's strong views aside, without dogs it would be impossible to farm much of New Zealand. On a high country station, well-trained working dogs become a musterer's best friend and most valuable asset.

Unlike the Aussies, who use blue heelers for cattle mustering which are pretty much treated like a 'jack of all trades', working dogs in New Zealand are generally either heading dogs or huntaways. The New Zealand heading dog works silently, using position and balance to pull sheep to their master, whereas a huntaway barks to drive sheep away. Putting a good stop whistle on them is essential so they only work on command and the mob can stay together and travel at a controlled pace. It is also important to put good sides on the dog so they understand when you want them to go left or right.

Untrained dogs with little control become liabilities to owners and everything around them. If a dog is particularly talented, strong-willed or simply doesn't understand what is required, there can be a big difference of opinion on how the job should be done. A string of four-letter words rings out across the hills. But generally, mustering is a relatively quiet affair as the musterers try to keep the sheep calm and avoid a dreaded split in the mob, bolt in the wrong direction or smother.

Top dog men test their skills and dogs against each other in the sport of sheepdog trialling. A keenly contested national sport, there are usually four events at each trial: the Long Head, the Short Head and Yard, the Zig-Zag Huntaway and the Straight Huntaway events. Working dogs that win official dog trials are recorded in the 'studbook' of the New Zealand Sheep Dog Trials Association. The association has no requirements on physical form or colour, as farmers are only interested in a dog's ability to work, and looks are of little concern.

The relationship between top dog trialists and their dogs is the key and once this breaks down you will hear that high country dog command, 'Wayleggo' ('you bastard', whispered under the trialist's breath). Which means it's all over and the sheep has had a win on the day. Out mustering in the high country, when you hear: 'Wayleggo, you bloody bastard, I'm going to get a hold of you,' it is a sure signal that the musterer has some problems coming up, and a team of dogs off down a gully chasing a single lamb is not a good sign.

James Mackenzie and his dog are possibly New Zealand's most legendary mustering team. In 1855 the Scotsman was imprisoned on a charge of stealing 1000 sheep from the Levels Station, South Canterbury.

Above: Once they go, they go. Merinos about to overpower this huntaway dog.   Shrek's Pet Hate **195**

Above: Dick Roy demonstrates yarding in Gore, watched by three generations of the Roy family, and Southland Collie Club president Rob Coulter. Shrek stands defiantly, front leg raised, trying to warn his three cousins before the gate is shut and it's too late.

Mackenzie's dog would go out at night and travel for miles to bring a mob of sheep back to him while he innocently played cards as the complete alibi.

My heading dog, nicknamed Evil, had developed some very bad habits that if I remember rightly I blamed on the breeder, Ginger Anderson. Although, I have to admit, the only one to blame was the trainer — myself. Shrek absolutely detested Evil as he could easily sense the dog had little respect for sheep.

My current heading dog Budge was well trained by a leading dog man named

Kerry Chittock. Budge has great balance and naturally positions himself well in relation to me and the mob. He also has a quite determined nature and is a joy to work.

If there is no sheep work during the day Budge will spend hours just quietly eyeballing and working the hens or ducks in the backyard by Shrek's house. He has the utmost respect for Shrek; and never have any of my dogs walked into the

Above: 'You're not such a bad bloke, Dick — without that dog of yours.'

ram shed uninvited.

Heather had a way of rubbing salt in the wound with the name Budge and nicknamed him Budget, as she felt I had paid far too much money for him! Even though it meant Heather missed out on a new ride-on lawnmower, I still believe Budge was worth every cent.

A good friend of mine, PL Anderson, has a dog called Brandy, a long-haired brindle huntaway that has a personality very similar to his owner — a bit of a

hard case. In their spare time, PL and Brandy go over to McRaes' at Glendhu Bay near Wanaka and run sheepdog demonstrations to entertain loads of Japanese tourists. PL will demonstrate his heading-dog skills, bringing the three sheep to him, then its Brandy's turn to take them away.

Brandy will walk along quickly behind the sheep without barking. The Japanese become quite agitated by this behaviour as their interpreter has told them all the different virtues between heading dogs and huntaways. Then for a bit of a laugh PL gives the command 'Konnichiwa' (Japanese for 'Good afternoon') at which Brandy's head goes back and he lets out his 500-decibels bark, scaring the hell out of the tourists.

'Aw, he very clever dog. Speak Japanese,' say the tourists.

Above: Mimi says goodbye to Shrek as he is being filmed for Japanese television.   Shrek's Pet Hate **199**
Shrek's thinking, 'I'll sort you out when we get back, little dog'.

The only problem for PL is that at dog trials Brandy often gets confused between English and Japanese.

Another local farmer in the Lindis Pass at Shirlmar Station, nicknamed Red-headed Gnome, has five dogs — four too many — and they are all supposed to be mind readers. When out mustering, the team of dogs has been known to take over. A short little fellow, Gnome would start going red in the face until his whole head had turned bright red. The dogs would sense the situation just by the colour of his face and start heading for home, at which point Gnome would explode like a pressure cooker.

In all seriousness, the relationship between man, his dogs and his flock is very special and Gnome had one of the best flocks in Central Otago, a very well-run property that had been home to some very good dog men from time to time.

Another character is Ronnie Davidson from the Lindis Crossing, next door to Bendigo. Ronnie has five dogs, all yellow, that ride around on the back of his flat-deck Mazda truck, all untethered, which is highly illegal. His property also

Above: The last one-way bridge on the state highway to Queenstown, which crosses the Lindis River, near Bendigo. Once you add Ronnie's sheep and Japanese tourists to the maze of confusing signs, you either have a comedy or a calamity.

happens to be split on either side of the Lindis River, with a one-way bridge on the busy state highway in between. That bridge must surely soon become iconic as it is one of the last one-way bridges on a national highway in New Zealand.

Anyway, at one time Ronnie was also chairman of the local council and his dogs didn't get a lot of time off the chain, so when they had a chance they always set out to make the most of a run, constantly barking and dashing around. As you would expect it was always very exciting when Ronnie moved sheep along the highway and over the narrow one-way bridge. Yellow dogs would race around buses, campervans and rentals, all full of tourists trying to take photos of sheep and also of the unusual pack of yellow dogs.

Sheep aren't overly excited about crossing bridges, so you can imagine how thrilled Ronnie was when, finally getting a lead sheep to start crossing with the rest following, a campervan stops at the other end of the bridge and Japanese tourists pile out, cameras blazing.

Ronnie, like the Gnome, had a fuse about as long as one of Wong's sticks of dynamite. Unfortunately, the more enraged Ronnie became, the more entertainment the Japanese got. And by this time, a long row of vehicles would be lined up each side of the bridge enjoying the spectacle.

The yellow dogs were enjoying the attention and pats from the tourists that they missed during the week with Ronnie away at meetings, while the sheep were stringing back through the traffic to the paddock from which they had come. Meanwhile, Ronnie, jumping up and down with a big stick, was as close to doing a Maori haka as we get in the south. But you could soon see which Japanese understood English as they quietly got back into their vehicles, wound up the windows and locked the doors.

I don't think we have ever had to engage professional entertainment. The issue is usually getting these characters to go home.

Rural life in New Zealand is rich with such colourful characters. I don't think in all the years at Tarras we have ever had to engage professional entertainment. The issue is usually getting these characters to go home.

Chapter 13

The Power of Shrek's Story

It has always amazed me that people still derive so much pleasure from an old wether. We have 30-odd million sheep in New Zealand and apart from the occasional show sheep or family pet, they are creatures you rarely see up close unless you are a Japanese tourist stopping on the side of the road to take a photo.

Why would corporates pay more for a sheep to appear than they would for an All Black or top sportsman? A lot of commercial interests in New Zealand still envy the power of the Shrek story. The continued public fascination with Shrek's wellbeing and journey over the years, I have to admit, has been carefully orchestrated and kept alive. Like any brand or career of a sportsman or politician, it can be destroyed overnight by one bad public performance.

As the 'Father of Shrek' I have never let him out of my sight, feeding him personally every day, watching his everyday moods and health. I needed to know him this well as, when travelling or among crowds, there were always many things that could go wrong and end in disaster. I can understand how, while celebrity bodyguards seem to be relaxed and not doing a lot, they are in fact under constant intense pressure. I certainly feel the stress of it, even with an old sheep like Shrek! But his wellbeing and security are number one and we intend it to stay that way until his calling comes.

Many people, including my family, thought I was mad taking Shrek on the road for charity. But after the tremendous success of the first shearing, I could see a huge opportunity to help sick kids and their families by building the Shrek brand. The power of the story carried by this old wether is envied by marketers around the world.

I remember one time, a renegade Romney ewe found in the bush country of Tapanui was shorn at a school gala day in Southland. A special white pen was built with red carpet leading up to it and Theona, clad in blue satin and bows,

Left: The iconic Luggate Pub, near Wanaka, with young entrepreneurial proprietor Sarah Perriam, who understands only too well the power of Shrek the sheep's story.

awaited Shrek's arrival. Media headlines were: 'Will It Be Love at First Sight?' Bagpipers led Shrek across the field and a grand parade of dressed-up kids followed. Theona had arrived at the event in a trailer — something Shrek would never do — and was not in good condition. To make matters worse, poor Theona was not to Shrek's liking and he got into an immediate tussle with her in front of a large crowd. There was no way he was going to have an arranged marriage with a common Southland ewe of doubtful heritage.

Theona's owners did not understand the importance of the story. I certainly didn't get everything right, but I did realise how vital it was to take every opportunity to make Shrek different from common sheep by having him travel in style, live in his own house and wear a custom-made red coat. Fortunately, with this treatment, Shrek's confidence in public grew, as did his mana. He helped me a lot with his unique temperament — he certainly is one of a kind. Shrek allows children to climb all over him, although he is a little less trusting of teenagers, some of whom, Shrek considers, have a lot to learn about life and respect for

others, even though he is a sheep.

He quickly learnt to happily walk in front of me like a dog, and he always wears his branded red cover in public. This is his signature and only sometimes does he wear a carefully selected scarf for special provincial appearances. Once he wore his Otago rugby scarf to a gala day at Waikaia in Southland and we were both bloody lucky to get out of the place alive, such is the interprovincial rivalry in rugby. The smaller the province, the stronger it gets. Believe it or not, Southland, the complete underdog, won the Ranfurly Shield last year. I think the party is still going! Their story has a lot of parallels with Shrek and typifies New Zealand. It doesn't matter how small you are, the strength is in the struggle — a heritage all Kiwis possess.

Part of Shrek's appeal is that he is a rebel with little interest in following the rules, which is why he turns up in unexpected places like hospitals, icebergs, shopping centre openings and airport travel lounges.

I quickly learnt it was always important not to overexpose Shrek at events.

Children and adults alike will wait hours for an advertised appearance, for a chance to see and touch the celebrity. But after a short time they will be satisfied he is real and off they will go with their photos and memories. The secret is not to hang around long or leave Shrek tied up all day in a pen, otherwise he loses some of his attraction.

I see a lot of parallels between Shrek and American recording artist Lady Gaga. If you were to take all Lady Gaga's clothes off I am sure she would look like any other woman in a crowd of nudists. She is just an ordinary girl with bizarre clothes. Shrek has a unique temperament and personality for a sheep and, like Lady Gaga, is remembered for the red coat he wears, the name he carries and the way he performs in public.

Of course if Shrek was shorn and put in a paddock of 1000 sheep without his red coat on, the best trained stockman would find it very difficult to pick him out of the mob. The only thing that would give Shrek away is the fact that he doesn't see himself as a sheep and would immediately walk away from the mob and come back to me or children watching.

Shrek's marketing power was recently demonstrated when the Auckland Phil-

Above: Children from all parts of New Zealand want their picture taken with Shrek. Here, in Waikaia, Southland, they crowd together for a group photo.

harmonia Orchestra held a live auction to raise funds. Random House donated a prize of four hours at the Home of Shrek at Bendigo and a visit to his cave. A very good line-up of valuable items were on offer that sold for an average of $1500. Believe it or not, the visit to see Shrek fetched the top price of the day at $5500. Tragically, in textile terms, this is more value than a farmer would get off 1000 of Shrek's strong-wool brethren.

But the Haddons from Auckland described their visit to see Shrek as being one of the most valuable and memorable experiences they have ever had. Again it was not just Shrek but his story that was the main attraction, delivered as a unique package of hospitality, exclusivity and the unforgettable location.

I will never forget the 100-year-old lady at the Winton Retirement Home who just couldn't believe it when Shrek marched into the living area and straight up to her for a happy birthday nuzzle. 'I never dreamed I would get to meet him,' she said.

Another time, Shrek popped into the retirement home in Frankton to visit a friend of mine, Frank, formerly of Nokomai Station. Frank is one of New Zealand's great ambassadors in farming and I will never forget the look on his face when

Shrek arrived in the lounge. Actively interested in everything, but particularly sheep and wool, Frank's eyes lit up and he immediately assessed Shrek's stance and composure. 'He's got a straight back,' Frank said, 'And look at how square he is over the back end.' Frank was highly excited that this animal was not only a celebrity but a fine example of what a sheep should look like in the eyes of a very experienced judge.

I must admit that if Shrek had been found 20 years earlier his story would have been very different. Shrek certainly wasn't the only woolly found on Bendigo over the years and none of the others have had such a long and luxurious life! I have been asked many times how as a farmer I became what many regard to be an entrepreneur and marketer. My view is that it is in the blood.

New Zealand, the home of Shrek, is blessed with every possible unique attribute one could wish for in marketing. It is small, surrounded by a big blue ocean, full of friendly people living in a clean and picturesque environment. It is a South Pacific paradise.

My Mates Call Me Shrek

Many people say they can see Shrek in me and I say, 'Go away — Shrek's a renegade.'

But it is quite interesting that whenever I am travelling in New Zealand, and being introduced to total strangers, someone with me will say, 'You probably know John Perriam.'

'Not really but nice to meet you, John.'

'He's from Bendigo Station.'

'That rings a bell.'

'He's the Father of Shrek, the sheep.'

'Oh my god, you really mean that?'

I confess to feeling a touch of pride every time, knowing that Shrek's story has gone so deep into a nation's consciousness, adding value to tourism and the national economy. A lot of my mates just call me Shrek now.

Cartoon by Murray Webb.

Cure Kids ambassador Lizzie McKay and Josie.

Josie couldn't believe her luck when Americans paid $35,000 for this painting, donated by Peter Beadle, courtesy of Shrek, to Cure Kids.

Cure Kids Chairman Roy Austin with Josie and Shrek on tour in Auckland.

Shrek and me doing our bit to promote bike safety.

The Life of Shrek
Cure Kids on the road

Above: This is what we call 'traffic' down south.

Chapter 14

Losing the Mother of Shrek

When Shrek was captured at the top of Bendigo, unbeknown to us, my wife Heather had cancer. The large malignant eye melanoma was not diagnosed for several months after Shrek was found but photos taken by the media clearly show Heather had a problem with her eye. Her flickering sight was first diagnosed as a possible detached retina but later confirmed as a melanoma taking up almost two thirds of her right eye.

We were busy with Shrek fundraising to help children with life-threatening diseases such as cancer. Now we knew first hand the disease had no boundaries, and Heather's diagnosis only strengthened our resolve to do all we could to raise money to fund vital medical research.

The day after the tumour was diagnosed in Dunedin we returned to Bendigo very depressed. It seemed there was no choice but to remove the eye. But word of Heather's predicament spread quickly on the local bush telegraph and we got a call from a stranger who told us a Californian eye specialist, Chuck McBride, happened to be visiting Tarras. He was looking for vineyard land and had heard about our dilemma via our local land agent. Chuck knew a world-leading eye melanoma surgeon, Dr Devron Char, at the UC Davis facility near Sacramento. Maybe he could help. So the next Sunday we were on a plane headed to the United States.

We were told there was a 98 per cent chance Dr Char could save Heather's eye using a proton beam created by a massive cyclotron that had been used to split the atom in World War Two and brought that terrible world conflict to an end. The same technology had been adapted to peacetime uses such as treating eye melanomas. After a week's preparation Heather underwent the treatment.

It appeared to be successful and for nearly three years we had to return to the US every six months for check-ups. The silver lining for Heather was getting to know many wonderful people and visit places such as the Napa Valley, renowned

for its wine production. These experiences sowed ideas for the development of our Bendigo wine sub-region, which has been so successful and of which we are very proud.

We were so confident the final check-up would be all clear that I stayed back in New Zealand getting stock ready for the Cromwell merino sales — a big event on our farming calendar. I got the call from the US while I was at the sale, just after Bendigo had received a top price for its annual draft ewes, such are the highs and lows in life. I was on a plane to the US the next day to be with Heather as she went through the very painful and difficult process of having her eye removed in a foreign country without the benefit of our social welfare-based hospital system. To the credit of Dr Char, there was no charge for the operation.

For the next three years I could say life went on as normal but life at Bendigo is never normal as it is a very busy place. Shrek wasn't helping normality much as he continued to attract huge public interest and was in hot demand to appear at events all over the country. Heather adapted to her glass eye extremely well and

Above: Heather always loved having a laugh with her staff and anyone who walked in the door.

put up with all the usual jokes: 'We will keep an eye out for you!' and she always said, 'I left my eye in San Francisco!' Heather loved people and people loved her so, just the same as before, she threw herself into the little Merino Shop and the many organisations she either led or mentored.

She continued to have health check-ups and everything seemed fine. But then, in late 2009, Heather went to her local GP at Wanaka because she didn't feel

well. That's when we got the devastating news. Tests detected tumours on Heather's liver. The diagnosis needed to be confirmed by a CAT scan in Dunedin, but we were advised she only had a short time to live.

When we got back from Wanaka the boys Daniel and Stewart were in the yard by the helicopter talking. She told them straight away and then broke the news to Christina, which was even more difficult

Above: Heather thoroughly enjoyed planning the look of the Tarras renovations.

Losing the Mother of Shrek **217**

because the two were very close.

After that, Heather and I walked into the Bendigo homestead kitchen and stood staring out the bi-fold windows at the hills of Bendigo that had been our life for the past 30 years. We were both in the strange vacuum only people who have been through it can describe. Then, in front of our eyes, a white rabbit hopped out of the garden and sat in front of us on the lawn. Of all the hundreds of thousands of rabbits that have come and gone on Bendigo during the last 30 years, I had never seen a pure white one, let alone on the lawn in front of the kitchen window. We were too dumbfounded to say much as we both looked at each other. Being very religious, Heather thought someone had sent a sign or was calling.

The visit to Dunedin the following Tuesday confirmed the worst. The oncologist sat us down as a family and delivered the terrible news that there was nothing conventional medicine could do for Heather. She had only a short time to live. The kids were horrified at his negativity and immediately nicknamed him Dr Death. Later that day, back at Bendigo, Heather said to me, 'John, I think this is going to be our biggest fight yet.' How right she was.

News of Heather's prognosis went through heartland New Zealand like a

Left: The grandkids, Lucy, Ferg and Olly with Shrek inside the House of Shrek, Tarras. **Above**: It was Heather's dream to have her own lolly shop in Tarras.

Losing the Mother of Shrek **219**

thunderstorm. Everybody was in disbelief, but the book *Dust to Gold* had told of all our struggles in earlier life and I think people thought the Perriam family were invincible and would overcome this challenge too.

Heather's dream had always been to redevelop the shops at little Tarras village, transforming it into a unique destination for tourists and locals alike. Over the years she had nearly driven me mad talking about her ideas for the country store, wine cellar, merino clothing retailing and even a Shrek information centre to display all the souvenirs stored in Shrek's office back at the House of Shrek. Whenever we travelled she'd spot coffee shops, general stores, plant nurseries and so on, and she would always say, 'Wouldn't it be great to do this at Tarras!'

Incredibly, six months before Heather became ill again we had decided to go ahead with the redevelopment, selling our section in Wanaka to finance the project.

Heather's dream had always been to redevelop the shops at little Tarras village.

Despite it being a difficult market, the section had sold on day one. Things just kept falling into place to make this project happen. The week after the section sold, Heather came into the homestead and said, 'You wouldn't believe this but Dave and Raewyn have turned up in their motor home.' They had done some renovation work on our homestead five years previously.

Dave said, 'Have you got any odd jobs about the station?'

'Yes,' I replied. 'The redevelopment of Tarras.'

'Holy hell!' said Dave.

For years Heather and I had been hoarding treasures for Tarras in the Bendigo woolshed. It was time for the heavy kauri shop counters from a Takaka drapery, enormous butcher's block, old shelving, church doors, theatre seats and other treasures to head down the road to Tarras. Dave scouted all the demolition outlets in the lower South Island and overnight turned the back yard at Bendigo into a joinery restoration shop. His motto is 'just do it', much to the annoyance of the local council building inspector who red-carded Dave off the job for his imaginative use of old materials and beams.

My family had refused to accept the oncologist's prognosis and had set about looking at alternative options for Heather. Between us all we had the Tarras village redevelopment completed on the day before Heather started her new cancer treatment in Christchurch. There was no time for a grand opening and it

Above: Christina's shop at Tarras. Her fashion label has taken merino products to new heights in the fashion industry, creating clothes from 100% merino wool, from Shrek's Kiwi cousins.

Above: Heather holds up the Tarras church kneeler, made from 100% merino wool, that she made. The kneelers were a Tarras community project that Heather really enjoyed.

was a sad day when Dave and Raewyn pulled out in the big motor home bound for the Bay of Islands.

As conventional biochemistry methods offered no hope for Heather we all agreed as a family to turn to the world of biophysics. This complicated technology involves the use of a frequency-loaded plate that rebalances blood cells and allows the body to optimise its own healing ability to remove toxins. This in turn increases the oxygen saturation levels in the blood and balances the pH levels to slightly alkaline.

There have been a lot of great success stories but for whatever reason it was not to be for Heather. However our whole family has a strong conviction that in time biophysics will play a major role in overcoming this disease that has become the curse of our society.

Led by Christina, we carried hope and fought the disease every way we knew. Heather had always yearned to live by the sea so we rented a house near Sumner overlooking the ocean and city. Christina shielded Heather from any negativity that might hinder her recovery and refused to let her mother indulge her sweet tooth. Ironically, a feature of the Tarras development was provision for an icecream parlour and lolly shop. It's all about balance, they say.

The day Heather passed away was 5 February 2010. That day the world changed forever for our family at Bendigo. Heather may have become affectionately known as the 'Mother of Shrek', but to our family she was the rock, and to the wider community she was an inspirational role model. After two months of total conviction by all the family that we were winning the battle, Heather had a fall in the night and her system started to give up. Her spirit quietly slipped away with all the kids desperately trying to stop it, holding her in their arms. Despite her brave battle, Heather had finally passed away to another world.

For two days after she was embalmed, Heather stayed with us high up on the hills at Sumner overlooking the sea and city. As sad as it was, this was a wonderful time because it allowed us as a family to start to come to terms with our loss. Stewart and I then flew back to Queenstown with Heather and we travelled by hearse back to Bendigo.

On the way back from the airport, a young roadworks man with a 'stop go' sign stopped us, as they were blasting rock at the Nevis Bluff. Jim Harbrow, the undertaker, said 'Can't you see who we have got in the back?' The young guy went white and started stuttering, 'I'm very sorry but I have no authority to let you through.' To which Jim replied, 'What about asking that chap over there?'

Relieved he was off the hook, the young guy ran over to a big fella with an orange coat who came walking over. Explaining he had just lost his father the week before, the boss said to go for it so off Jim went with rocks falling off the face onto the road, straight past a huge row of startled traffic waiting on the other side. I told Jim that Heather would have really enjoyed that as she had always got peeved that, when we travelled with Shrek, he would be allowed through any situation, but without him we were treated just as human beings. Heather sure had the last laugh on Shrek there.

At Bendigo we had several evenings with close friends standing around Heather's coffin, laughing and crying about all the good old days. And during the days, close friends and the ever-so-loyal Merino Shop staff visited her. Even our cat Oliver would go in and sleep on her lap at night.

By the day of the funeral we were all emotionally drained after the two-month campaign to save Heather. The funeral was a massive affair with over 1000 people attending and 2000 sympathy cards received. Later, Kate Coughlan, editor of *NZ House & Garden* magazine, summed it up by saying Heather's funeral was the most uplifting occasion she had ever attended and she went away thinking about how to be a better person.

The service was held at the little Tarras church up on the hill where Heather had played the organ. Then the crowd drove to Bendigo for high tea and a musical concert on the front veranda. We released helium balloons and Heather's white pigeons, which disappeared towards the blue sky and hills of Bendigo beyond.

Above: Tarras village — once just a pee-and-pie-stop — is now a unique destination for many travellers.

It was a very spiritual moment, with a very emotional crowd watching.

Then, as the rest of the family departed with Heather for the private burial, the huge crowd linked arms in a human chain around the teardrop lawn in a symbol of human struggle against cancer. It stretched all the way down the driveway out to the highway while Heather's beloved bagpipes played. Our grandchildren were dressed in tartan. It was a fitting send-off and Heather would have been so proud.

At the service I spoke about the visit of the white rabbit. A mate of mine, Keith Sutton, was standing alongside a Maori lady in the long chain of friends. She had introduced herself as Miriama, one of Heather's bridesmaids. Miriama has a beautiful welcoming face, so it didn't matter that Keith didn't know her. He suggested to her that perhaps the white rabbit was like the Maori 'he kotuku rerenga tahi', which translates to 'the white heron flies this way but once'. She agreed because the saying is used when someone special comes by or when something unusual happens. But Miriama seemed more focused on the funeral party as it drew level, and on behalf of everyone she launched into her waiata tangi — a bridesmaid's salute to a lifetime friend. It was very special and startlingly so for many in the Pakeha throng.

The days that followed were very difficult, all of us trying to handle the waves

Above: Now that Christina is a manager, Mimi spends her days as a well-groomed village dog.

of emotion — me losing my soulmate and the kids losing 'the best mother in the world'. I remember walking into Shrek's shed, tears streaming down my face and letting him have it. 'Why are you still alive, when you are the most useless, worthless, four-legged bastard,' I raved. 'You've outlived my mother, my father and now Heather.' He stood right up to me, staring in disbelief, as if to say, 'It's not all about you, you know.'

And he was right. They say in emotional situations you take your frustration out on those who are closest to you. In hindsight my outburst was a little disappointing, but I apologised to Shrek the next day as I discovered the world keeps turning whether you like what happens in life or not. Life is such a gift and Heather had made the most of every day she was given.

Sadly Heather never had the chance to return to her beloved little village at Tarras before she died in Christchurch. But she left a proud legacy that Christina, family and staff are all working day and night to continue. Heather's dream that for years to come thousands of people will visit Tarras and enjoy the memory of shopping at this special little village in heartland New Zealand has come true.

The cancer that claimed her life seems to have become an epidemic in our society, striking with little warning in young and old. It changes the lives of not only those suffering the disease but also all those around them. My heart goes out to the countless New Zealanders fighting cancer or who have lost close friends

Above: Recycled church doors, opening to the blue Central Otago sky and brown hills of Tarras. As they say, 'When one door closes, another opens'.

228 Shrek: The story of a Kiwi icon

Above: A proud Shrek outside the House of Shrek in Tarras. I thought he was the only sheep in New Zealand to have his own house, but surely he has to be the only one with two!

or family to the disease. You are not alone and there are many good stories of people who have beaten it thanks to modern and so-called alternative methods as well as sheer determination.

We are very proud of the way our family carried hope and determination right until the end to beat the disease. The attempt to save Heather's eye rather than having it removed immediately may have ultimately cost her life. We will never know.

Since Heather died our whole family has changed the way we think, eat, drink and exercise. We have seen the world of drug companies and ambulances waiting at the bottom of the cliff and these days we intend to deal with things at the top of the cliff and encourage others to do the same.

I've had to get on with the hard reality of life without Heather. Not long after she passed away a friend suggested I join the gym in Wanaka. Having always been physically active on the station mustering and farming, I had never considered joining a gym before. But I must admit in recent years I have spent more time travelling to board meetings and less time farming and much of my fitness had dropped away. In a small community like Tarras, I knew I would probably get stick from the locals but after all we had been through, I thought, 'What the hell!'

So I discovered George, who runs the gym in Wanaka. I became convinced

Above: Sunset at Paihia, in the Bay of Islands.

he used to work for the Gestapo after an hour of him pushing me beyond my comfort zone. In my subconscious, he became 'George the bastard'. Actually, George is a good man but his routine doesn't vary, whether you are 26 or 66, but at the end of the day you are your own boss. It's a whole new way to get ready for the day ahead. I can see why gyms are among the fastest-growing businesses in New Zealand. It's great because we have to take responsibility for our own health and not leave it up to doctors and drug companies.

I've also taken to walking up the local Mt Iron. I have driven past it all my life, usually in a hurry to get to the accountant's or solicitor's and mentally planning my next entrepreneurial project. But the hour-long climb over the track with the dogs is free to all New Zealanders and visitors and would have to be the most invigorating thing I do, along with George and the gym. It puts a whole new meaning into the hot shower and good old cup of tea waiting at the end of it.

Our family has become painfully aware it is the simple things in life that are so precious, as well as making time for people — something Heather always had such a wonderful way of doing.

Heather Perriam made a dying wish that a trust be established at Tarras village for the specific purpose of helping those in need to confront and overcome cancer. When visiting the village, remember, with every purchase a small but important percentage of sales will go to this trust (administered by her children and special outside trustees). It was also Heather's wish that no funds will go towards the administration; instead it all goes directly to those in need.

'Right, back it up then, we're going to have to get him outta this crate.'

'Hey mate, I don't think it's going to fit.'

'What do you think the other passengers will think if we tell them the plane is going to be delayed while we wait for a sheep?!'

After the pilot makes the embarrassing announcement, and calls for the Father of Shrek to come to lend a hand, he sneaks a look for himself.

'You've had your fun, Shrek. The passengers have been waiting for 20 minutes now. One way or another, you are getting on this plane.'

Resigned to not being able to take off until Shrek is sorted, the pilot has a cunning plan — get a photo for the kids back home.

The Life of Shrek

It could only happen in New Zealand

Chapter 15

Shrek Goes on Holiday

After Shrek's last public shearing, at the top of Auckland's Sky Tower in 2008, he returned to live a quiet life in the luxurious House of Shrek. Life at Bendigo rolled on around him, one season following another, and he continued to receive visitors. But it seemed like something was missing.

It appeared retirement did not entirely suit this elderly super celebrity who loves people. In late 2009 I noticed he was becoming quite lethargic, showing little interest in everyday goings on — Heather's hens laying in his feed trough, the dog being let out every day and his routine feeding morning and night. He was very healthy but his alertness was fading.

All that changed in May 2010 when I decided to take him on tour to get fresh material for this book. Being a New Zealand icon himself, the idea was to take Shrek to iconic places and to meet iconic people. We'd get some great photos and stories and have a lot of fun along the way too.

I must confess, I was a bit nervous about taking such an old sheep far from home. Shrek is 14, going on 15 years old and he would be in the public eye. Heaven forbid if anything should happen to him while we were away — I'd have a full-time job responding to the letters to the editor in the *Otago Daily Times*.

Putting Shrek in the back of his Jeep to go visiting wasn't too much of a risk, but when I decided the tour should also include Auckland and Northland I knew we would be pushing the boundaries big time as that required several flights, a lot of driving and being away from home for five days. Any person remotely near Shrek's age in human years would be safely tucked up in the retirement home with the central heating at 30˚C.

I must confess, every time I waited for Shrek to come off a plane and left him with his billet for the night, it was with a tinge of anxiety. But Shrek needed stimulation and, as it turned out, the more places he visited and the more people he met, the brighter he seemed. There was an uncanny parallel with

older humans who remain active and have adventurous and enquiring minds, living life to the full.

The tour was supposed to be private but a sheep in a red coat does stand out and the media quickly got on to the story. Before we knew it, Shrek was appearing on national TV and a very friendly TV One reporter was revealing his plans for this book. The media love him, always have, always will. The story was a winner — yet again, Shrek got himself into virtually every New Zealand household at prime time.

The fun had begun before we even left Queenstown airport. Shrek's red-lined corporate box had disappeared from the airport storage area only three days earlier. A new box was quickly found and no one gave a second thought to the fact it was larger than the original one, although this was to cause an embarrassing incident later on.

Of course, Auckland was the place where Shrek was last shorn. When he had boarded a private jet for the return trip back to Bendigo, we had thought that

Above: Treaty House education officer Barbara Brown and Shrek at the Waitangi Treaty grounds, most likely the site of the first shearing by scissors in New Zealand.

would be his last visit to the Super City. Little did we realise he'd be back in two years looking for more adventure.

Shrek arrived at Auckland airport looking full of mischief and off we went to visit Eden Park — the home of The Blues rugby team. A new stand was being built for the 2011 Rugby World Cup so the place was strictly out of bound for visitors. The security guard at the front gate was totally unimpressed by our intention to get inside. We were about to give up when the guard asked, 'What's that animal in the back of the rental car?'

'That's Shrek,' said Josie, opening the door. Next thing we knew, the power of Shrek took over and head management were contacted. As luck would have it, Monday was a public holiday and the workforce were away. So Shrek the rugby supporter got a personal guided tour and photo taken with an All Blacks scarf on

Above: With Barbara Kuruleca outside Te Waimate Mission House, the site for the second signing of the Treaty of Waitangi.

Shrek Goes on Holiday **239**

the hallowed turf at Eden Park.

After that we decided it was time for a little shopping so we headed downtown and had a ride on one of the city's buses. Lunch was at a top restaurant, The Grove, then we headed to the Auckland Museum to look at the exhibits. Home that night was an exclusive gated home in Remuera, one of Auckland's wealthiest suburbs, where we enjoyed drinks and nibbles with the who's who of Auckland society.

Next day we headed for Northland and the Bay of Islands, which holds a very special place in Shrek's heritage. According to the book *A Short History of Sheep in New Zealand* by Richard Wolfe, the Reverend Samuel Marsden arrived at Rangihoua in the outer reaches of the Kerikeri Inlet with eight merino on 23 December 1814. A further 12 merino were then purchased by missionary William Hall and in 1817 they were all shifted to graze at Waitangi. However, as a result of a dispute with local Maori, some of them were shifted quickly to Marsden's second mission station at Kerikeri basin, which was set up in 1819.

Above: After so many interviews, Shrek no longer needs me to speak for him. Here he is, broadcasting live to the nation from the Auckland Museum.

A number were shorn at Waitangi so it is very likely to be the first place in New Zealand that merino shearing took place. These were not the first sheep to land in New Zealand, as Captain Cook had brought six to the country previously, taken on board at the Cape of Good Hope in South Africa. Only two had survived the voyage, and he landed the ram and ewe in May 1773 off the sailing ship *Resolution* at Ship Cove in the Marlborough Sounds. Unfortunately, those two died after eating poisonous plants. But eventually, others were introduced and they found their way to drier parts in the South Island.

To acknowledge the connection between Shrek and his pioneer cousins, Shrek had his photo taken at Waitangi in front of the Treaty House where, on 6 February 1840,

Above: A Maori welcome from Atarangi Norman at the old stone store in Kerikeri, the site where Shrek's first ancestors were established in New Zealand.

242 Shrek: The story of a Kiwi icon

Above: Shrek was a lot more comfortable about this picture than me, a farm boy in riding boots from down south.

the Treaty of Waitangi was first signed between Maori and the British Crown. He also posed for the camera at The Stone Store at Kerikeri basin, New Zealand's oldest surviving stone building, built 1832–36 as a mission storehouse.

Then it was time to head to the other coast to remember another New Zealand animal icon that loved human company. During the summer of 1955–56, Opo the bottlenose dolphin became famous throughout New Zealand for playing with the children of the small town of Opononi on the Hokianga Harbour. Unfortunately, Opo was killed, but she is immortalised by a song, films and memorial statue in Opononi.

The next icon on Shrek's whirlwind tour of Northland was a visit to the great Tane Mahuta on the Kauri coast. The largest known living kauri tree, this Lord of the Forest is over 50 metres high and is estimated to be between 1250 and 2500 years old. A visit to the Kauri Museum at Matakohe tells a fascinating story of the pioneering days through the use of kauri timber and kauri gum.

After a very successful tour it was time to head back down south to the snow. But it was not to be as straightforward as we had expected. At the airport Shrek duly hopped into his box, which was weighed ready for loading in the cargo hold, no problem. Stephen and I decided to have breakfast at the lounge until the passengers were called to board. Walking along the glass corridor to board we noticed a sea of green coats below the 737 jet and a lot of activity around a certain box with Shrek peering out. Oh no, the new box wouldn't fit in this plane!

With all passengers and bags loaded, the ground crew had a major issue on their hands. The pilot announced to the 130 passengers on board there was a technical problem with Shrek's corporate box. Next thing, out came Shrek in his red coat, wondering what all the excitement was about. While the ground crew waited for authorised personnel to sort out the issue, they started taking photos of themselves with Shrek, who by now was out of his crate. Not wanting to miss out, the pilot slid open the window in the cockpit and, through a cunning manoeuvre, started taking photos on his cellphone.

Then, over the loudspeaker, I heard the announcement, 'Could the Father of Shrek come to security immediately, please?'

'That's you,' said Stephen, who was having a field day recording the event.

So I put on a green vest and went out on the tarmac where I found Shrek happily holding up the flight. But he could see by the look in my eye that the party was over. He was going onto the plane come hell or high water and he knew it. The best solution was to turn the crate on its side to squeeze it through the door and then put Shrek back inside. Shrek was a little bemused about the new sideways arrangement but soon we were off, much to the relief of the ground crew. Of course I had to walk the gauntlet down the aisle to row 29 while the passengers stared at me — how embarrassing. Stephen had long since boarded and pretended not to know me. It was with a great deal of relief that I took my seat for the trip home to Central Otago.

In the South Island we visited more high country icons, such as the historic 34-stand stone shearing shed at Morven Hills in Central Otago and the bronze memorial to musterers' dogs on the shores of Lake Tekapo by the Church of the Good Shepherd.

Sadly, some icons don't last forever, and to mark the end of an era, Shrek accepted an invitation to tea from the Williamson family at Birchwood Station up the Ahuriri Valley near Omarama. The Williamsons had farmed Birchwood for generations, but the property had been purchased by the Crown for conservation purposes. In just a few weeks they were to leave their family home; but the tea party was a great occasion and Shrek enjoyed playing with the latest generation of young red-headed Williamsons.

As part of the South Island tour we also paid a visit to Shane Nyhon at Milford Sound. A high country musterer turned crayfisherman, Shane had mustered Shrek's block on Bendigo the year before Shrek was captured. He and the Bendigo stock manager had been given the slip by the wily wether, but Shane also reminded me I was there for that muster too, as well as the one the year before. After Shrek was found Shane had traded his musterer's hill pole and dogs in to go back fishing with his father Denis. Business has never been better for him and he reckons Shrek's capture had a silver lining after all.

For old times' sake, Denis and Shane offered Shrek and me a day out crayfishing and viewing *The tour was supposed to be private but a sheep in a red coat does stand out.*

the magnificent Sounds waterfalls and birdlife. It was Shrek's first time out at sea in a boat and he quickly had a lot of sympathy for his ancestors who sailed from the other side of the world. It took a little while for Shrek to work out the moving deck he was standing on wasn't exactly connected to the solid rocky mountains where he had hidden for five years.

I quickly came to the same conclusion as Shrek — that some people and animals just aren't cut out for the sea. Sheep and high country farmers enjoy the experience of being at sea for very limited periods of time. After that, things become problematic. Sea sickness was not so bad for Shrek because even though he only has four teeth left in his head, they are all his. Mine got knocked out at an early age playing rugby, riding rodeo and talking when I should have been listening. So, as the swell got heavier, I knew that if the trip had gone on much longer, my false teeth and I were in for some trouble! Especially seeing as Stephen was on board with his damned camera! But he did capture the magic of Milford beautifully.

Actually, there were only two times on the entire tour when Shrek got upset — both related to the presence or scent of a dog. Once was at Paihia in the Bay of Islands. Our hosts had a very nice lifestyle block that had previously been used as a canine boarding establishment. Although Shrek's sleeping arrangements were very comfortable he obviously detected the scent of dogs from way back and he spent a very restless night. The other incident was down in Southland at the Gore dog trials. He became quite indignant at seeing three of his mates being penned in front of him by a very well-trained dog. Standing defiantly with no lead, stomping his front leg, he tried to encourage his three cousins to rebel against the dog, but to no avail.

The tour with Shrek was a huge success, giving him a new love of life and reminding me what a wonderful gem of Mother Nature we New Zealanders are privileged to live in. Without exception, overseas visitors who are fortunate enough to have time to fully explore New Zealand go home enriched with experiences very much related to the landscape and the people they meet. I don't know how many times I have heard the brash budget tourist say, 'My god, we done that little sucker of a country in two days.' How wrong they are, and how wonderful it is to see a major shift towards discerning visitors taking the time to properly experience the attractions and stories of New Zealand that will live in their memories for the rest of their lives.

Touring with Shrek also reminded me that New Zealanders have an inner pride about their country, and that includes Shrek. Young and old — from corporate types to heartland rural communities — all have an instant sense of pride and ownership of Shrek, stopping to take a photo of him or, more importantly, get one of themselves with him. If he were a well-known politician or human celebrity, I am sure people would act quite differently, pretending not to notice or stare as they walked on. It gives me a great deal of satisfaction that Shrek's story helps close the gap between city and rural New Zealand.

uring his time at Bendigo, Shrek has lived through many highs and lows and along the way has become very much a part of the family and our story. He may be 'just a sheep', but he has given us a new way of thinking. He's taught us that life doesn't owe you a living and, as depressing and impossible as a situation may seem, there is always hope — so make the most of every opportunity. He sure did — from the moment Ann spotted him on the top of Bendigo. And of course there is all the money he has raised for charity and the enjoyment he has given countless millions of people, which is something money can't buy.

Shrek's incredible journey could only have happened in New Zealand, because it is a very special place. This book will hopefully act to further immortalise Shrek's story, and once and for all satisfy all the doubters — yes, as incredible as it is, the Shrek of today is the same sheep as the one found on the top of Bendigo six years ago. And what's more, there will never be another one because he is totally unique. Thanks, Shrek, it's been a great ride and a real privilege.

Shrek poses in front of this sailing ship at Waitangi, pondering the long voyage his ancestors would have had from the other side of the world.

The Treaty House, Waitangi.

The Kauri Museum at Matakohe, with museum patron Mavis Smith in June 2010. Mavis was 99 at the time.

Shrek meets Mary Hohaia outside this classic Kiwi hot food caravan.

Tane Mahuta, the largest known living kauri tree in New Zealand.

Shrek looks over the plaque that commemorates the signing of the Treaty of Waitangi, one of the most significant moments in New Zealand's short history.

The Life of Shrek

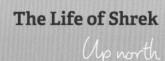

Up north

Above: Shrek sampling native fern in the Kauri forest reserve. He had a lot of sympathy for his early ancestors, but enjoyed a fern leaf or two while DOC weren't watching.

Skipper Shane Nyhon and his girlfriend, Nelly, aboard the Southern Legend in the Milford Sound.

At the Homer Tunnel, Shrek cautiously eyes up a kea. Shrek has heard from his merino cousins about kea attacks on sheep on high country stations.

A mollymawk glides through the Milford air.

Taking in the classic scenery of Milford Sound.

When we couldn't get close enough to shore to get Shrek off the boat safely in a conventional way, the fisherman came up with a better idea.

The Life of Shrek
Way down south

Above: Shrek and Regan checking the crayfish aboard the
Southern Legend in Milford Sound.

This is the last will and testament of Shrek, New Zealand hermit merino.

I leave all royalties from my book to Cure Kids in the hope that this money will continue to assist them to fund through medical research ways to save lives of children not only in New Zealand but throughout the world.

I also wish that my funeral service be held at the Church of the Good Shepherd, Tekapo, and that my body or ashes be buried or spread at the top of Mt Cook, New Zealand's highest mountain. For from there I can watch over the South Island high country, home of my ancestors for 150 years, and a place I have loved during the special lifetime I have been privileged to share with so many New Zealanders.

As long as the stars shine in the sky it will be a symbol of hope to the generations to follow.

Signed

Shrek